Chase Jesus
with all that
you are!
Jacki C King

The Calling of Eve

THE

# Calling
# of Eve

How the
Women of the Bible
Inspire the Women
of the Church

## Jacki C. King

THOM S. RAINER, SERIES EDITOR

TYNDALE
**MOMENTUM**®

*A Tyndale nonfiction imprint*

Visit Tyndale online at tyndale.com.

Visit Tyndale Momentum online at tyndalemomentum.com.

*Tyndale*, Tyndale's quill logo, *Tyndale Momentum*, and the Tyndale Momentum logo are registered trademarks of Tyndale House Ministries. Tyndale Momentum is a nonfiction imprint of Tyndale House Publishers, Carol Stream, Illinois.

*The Calling of Eve: How the Women of the Bible Inspire the Women of the Church*

Designed by Ron C. Kaufmann

All the examples and stories in this book are true. Names and some specific details have been modified to protect the privacy of the individuals involved.

For information about special discounts for bulk purchases, please contact Tyndale House Publishers at csresponse@tyndale.com, or call 1-855-277-9400.

**Library of Congress Cataloging-in-Publication Data**
A catalog record for this book is available from the Library of Congress.

ISBN 978-1-4964-6208-4

Printed in the United States of America

| 28 | 27 | 26 | 25 | 24 | 23 | 22 |
|----|----|----|----|----|----|----|
| 7  | 6  | 5  | 4  | 3  | 2  | 1  |

*To Josh and the Boys*

*Josh,*
*You have been the steady and faithful voice cheering me on through all the seasons of life. I would not be the woman I am today if it weren't for you. I love the team that we are. I love you deeply.*

*Haddon, Leland, and Amos,*
*The depth of joy you bring me is unmatched. You've helped me learn so much about God and his love for us. I am so proud and grateful to be your mom.*

# Contents

# 1

# Searching
# for Womanhood

It was a typical Sunday morning at church. Lots of smiles in the lobby as people stood in small clusters, sipping coffee and visiting before the service.

When the service began, groups of friends and families hustled into the sanctuary, some arriving late with their coffee in one hand and their Bible in the other. We sang. We prayed. We listened intently to the message.

This particular message presented the gospel, including an invitation to come forward and surrender to Christ. At the conclusion of the message, the plan was for all our ministers and pastors to stand at the front of the sanctuary to pray with those who felt the Spirit's prompting. As the minister to women for our church, I would be among them. When the music began to play and I started to make my way to the front, I noticed that our children's minister seemed to be missing. *She must have gotten pulled away into one of the classrooms*, I thought. This left me as the only woman standing at the front, an experience I'd had many times.

As we began to sing, people started moving through the aisles, asking for prayer. I scanned the congregation and made eye contact with a nine-year-old girl named Langley. I smiled at her as she tugged at her mom's shirt and pointed to me. I wondered what she was saying. Then I caught the eye of one of our teenage girls, Haven, and her younger sister, Reese. They had the same kind of look, both curious and longing, and then they smiled. Next my eyes landed on several of our college girls that I lead in a small group. They broke the serious vibe with silly faces, and one tossed up a heart shape with her hands. Trying to keep my composure and fight the urge to shoot back an equally goofy face, I smiled and shared a quick wink. These were souls and faces I loved to see each week, and God was doing remarkable things in and through them. And I had the privilege of a front-row seat.

As I drove home that day, I couldn't stop thinking about Langley's bright eyes and smile. I had vivid memories of what it was like to be her age and in church almost every Sunday. Mrs. Vicki was my Sunday school teacher, and she faithfully taught our class week after week using flannel board Bible characters and coloring sheets—the cutting-edge technology of the day.

Mrs. Susan was the faithful piano player for our worship services. She was one of the quietest women I had ever met, but her fingers flew across the piano keys at crazy speeds when she played the old hymn "Since Jesus Came into My Heart."

Then there was Mrs. Blair, who gathered us elementary school-girls together every Sunday afternoon at 4:00 to teach us about different missionaries around the world.

I considered Mrs. Dot an adopted grandma. She and her husband, Brother Tommy, gave me a hug each week as I entered the building. Then Mrs. Dot made her way to the infant room to rock crying babies and change dirty diapers, a role in which she served for decades.

I loved these women and their smiles. I loved how they knew so much about the Bible and God. I loved how faithful they were, that I could rely on them to be there for me and others, ready to share hugs and stories that pointed my heart to Jesus. These were the women who made me fall in love with the church. It was just who they were. It was how they served. It was how they led.

There was never a question in my mind that women were a part of God's Kingdom and mission, simply because from my earliest memories I was surrounded by women. It wasn't until I was a bit older that I began to experience doubts and to question where I fit in as a woman in the church.

## Where Do I Fit In?

I was a loud and energetic kid. I mean, really loud. (I blame it on being Cuban.) I was also an off-the-charts extrovert. I constantly got in trouble for talking in school and spent a good bit of time in detention after chemistry class because I was way more interested in catching up with my friends than in anything to do with molecules and periodic tables. I wasn't a social butterfly; I was more like a social June bug. Butterflies are winsome and full of grace as they flit between social settings. June bugs, on the other hand, are a bit awkward, clumsily flying into things. And with their loud buzzing, everybody knows they're coming.

Teachers and coaches told me I was a natural leader, although I sometimes led people in the wrong direction. I remember the stern voice of my youth minister when he called once to reprimand me. Apparently I had not set a good example for the younger students when I enlisted them to join me in egging the car of an ex-boyfriend. Some might have considered it vandalism, but I preferred to think of it as a team-building activity. In sports, I was the team captain and the person everyone relied on to rally the team when we were behind and in a funk. I led the cheers, and I led the prayers.

I wasn't that great with kids, and I was horrible at crafts. While my friends earned summer money babysitting, I opted to mow lawns and walk dogs. I loved competition, hated glitter and anything pink, and had more questions than answers when it came to life and the Bible.

I think as young girls we were always looking ahead and trying to decide who we wanted to be. That's why sports heroes and fashion models always piqued our interest. So when I looked at the Bible and the church, I naturally looked at the women and wondered who was most like me and who I could become.

Unfortunately, it seemed like the only time women were ever talked about in church, the topic was submission—how Eve messed up by eating the fruit, or that part about how women are to learn silently with a gentle spirit. None of these were bad or wrong, but they sure seemed like a narrow set of lenses on life, womanhood, and leadership in the church. And none of them felt like me—remember, I'm the June bug!

I loved the church. I adored Jesus and wanted to serve him. But I had no idea what that might look like for me. I wondered, *Did God mess up? How much of me was too strong and needed to be reined in? Would I need to always defer and give in? Did being a woman who pleased God mean being a woman who was not like me?*

As a young woman, I thought I was the only one who wrestled with such questions and insecurities. But as I began to have conversations with other women leaders over the years, I discovered that many of them also had struggles with identity, expectations, and purpose. And yet, when I shared my frustrations and questions with other women leaders, it became clear that many of us had spent more energy trying to live up to our own vague notions of what a biblical woman was supposed to be than actually studying what the Bible says about women. There is a difference.

## What Is a Biblical Woman?

Depending on where you grew up, the faith tradition you were a part of, and the home you were raised in, the phrase "biblical womanhood" may have a positive or negative connotation. Your mind might go immediately to the talking points of roles and order of creation. Or you might think of your favorite woman of the Bible and the wisdom you've gleaned from her story. The first thing that comes to mind for me is the Proverbs 31 woman.

I used to loathe the Proverbs 31 woman. She was the one who set an unachievably high bar of womanhood and had all her ducks in a row. With ease and the most gracious demeanor, she always kept the plates of womanhood spinning. She never lost her cool or her calm smile. At least, that's how everyone I knew described her.

If she was the model woman, I was completely lacking—even on my best day—in whatever, apparently, was expected of me. In Bible college, I remember the guys talking about trying to find their "P31 wife." Not only was I not her; I didn't *want* to be her. It wasn't until many years later, when I was asked to speak on Proverbs 31 at a women's event, that my thinking began to change. And that was because my *perception* of the Proverbs 31 woman was finally replaced by an understanding of who she actually represents.

What if I told you that the Proverbs 31 woman isn't really a woman at all? That when we view chapter 31 through the lens of the entire book of Proverbs—a collection of wisdom writings that often portray wisdom as a woman—we see that it is written as an oracle of a queen who is giving advice to her son about what it would look like to be *married to wisdom.*

The Proverbs 31 woman has been used as a checklist of expectations for women who aspire to become good wives and homemakers, with a variety of skills to master—everything from bringing home the bacon to running her own business. However, a closer look at the chapter reveals a creatively written Hebrew acrostic poem that uses the illustration of a woman who is known and used by God in all different ways and who exhibits the virtues of God to everyone around her.

Seen in this context, Proverbs 31 is relevant for *everyone* who seeks to be transformed and used by God. Once I understood this, the seemingly unattainable high bar of womanhood became instead a celebration of character, grace, compassion, and strength. This was something I very much wanted after all!

In Proverbs 31:11-31, the queen details a list of attributes she champions in a woman:

She is trustworthy (verse 11).
She is a hard worker (verses 13-15, 17, 19).
She is resourceful and savvy (verses 16, 18).
She is compassionate; she sees and cares for the needy
    (verse 20).
She is strong (verses 17, 25).
She is wise (verse 26).
She is loved (verse 28).
She fears the Lord (verse 30).

I am especially intrigued by the attribute of "strength" on this list, which doesn't always come through in our English translations. But in the original Hebrew text, the strength of the Proverbs 31 woman is conveyed using three different words: *khayil*, *'oz*, and *'amets*.

The first word appears in verse 10: "Who can find a virtuous and capable wife? She is more precious than rubies." The Hebrew word translated as "virtuous" is *khayil*, which is often used in a military context to describe valor, strength, and might. It is used again in verse 29—"There are many virtuous [*khayil*] and capable women in the world, but you surpass them all!"—to complete the parallel, chiastic structure of the poem. It's like there are two bookends, with the verses in between displaying how the Proverbs 31 woman brings virtue, strength, and beauty to the world when *khayil* is the drumbeat of her life.

The second Hebrew word that means "strong" appears in verse 17: "She is energetic and strong." *'Oz* means strong, bold, or loud. Did you catch that? To be loud can be a reflection of strength! This clause literally means "she girds her loins with strength." This is a very masculine descriptor of our P31 woman. This word is repeated in verse 25: "She is clothed with strength [*oz*] and dignity."

The third word is used at the end of verse 17: "She is energetic and strong, a hard worker." The Hebrew word translated "hard worker" is *'amets*. It means to be courageous, firm, and solid.

Together, these words that convey strength paint a picture of a woman who merits the same respect as a decorated warrior. She leverages her strength for the good of others and for the king she serves.

So, what is a biblical woman according Proverbs 31? Verse 30 summarizes it well: She is "a woman who fears the LORD."

## A Woman Who Fears the Lord

To understand what it means to fear the Lord, it's important to know something about the Hebrew word for "fear" that is used here—*yare*. The verb *yare* means to cause astonishment and awe, to make afraid, or to have reverence.

One aspect of *yare* is similar to the fear you might experience when confronted with a snake or a skunk out in the woods. While walking down a nature trail, you might be terrified of being bitten or sprayed, but there's an element of respect and humility in your fear. You recognize that you are at the mercy of a creature you cannot control. But unlike meeting a skunk or a snake, when we encounter our heavenly Father, our inability to control a perfect and holy God is actually for our good and benefit. This is one aspect of *yare*. It isn't just being terrified or afraid; it also has an element of respect and humility.

Another aspect of *yare* is more about wonder and awe. I experienced something like this as a kid when I spent a couple of weeks each summer at my aunt and uncle's farm in the Texas Panhandle. There would be these huge thunderstorms we could see coming for miles as they rolled in. The clouds turned from fluffy cotton ball–like puffs to huge wall-like structures of swirling white and gray. I loved watching the giant streaks of light flash across the sky and feeling the rumbles of thunder deep in my chest. It was beautiful. It was grand. It was way bigger than me and completely out of my control.

It is this mix of respect, humility, awe, and wonder that is the fear of the Lord. It stops you in your tracks, and it humbles you with the reminder that you can't control God or box him in. The God who made the planets and thunderstorms is the same God who reaches down to reveal himself through his Word. In his presence, we experience holy fear in the form of awe, wonder, and utter respect for who he is, the power he holds, and the humility he requires.

When I am teaching my kids or describing to women what it means to fear the Lord, I always think of the Narnia story. I love the scene in *The Lion, the Witch, and the Wardrobe* when young Lucy first hears about Aslan, whose character is a strong and powerful lion. She asks, "Is he—quite safe? I shall feel rather nervous about meeting a lion." And Mr. Beaver replies, "Who said anything about safe? 'Course he isn't safe. But he's good. He's the King, I tell you."[1]

To fear the Lord is to acknowledge that while God is all-powerful, all-knowing, and absolutely sovereign, he chooses in his grace to make himself known to us. We approach him with a healthy reverence because we understand that he is our Creator and we were made for him. He is our Father, and we are his children. He is our King, and we are his servants.

Over the years that I've ministered to women, I've noticed there tends to be two misguided images we have when we think about what it means to fear the Lord. I call them the angry dad and the fairy godmother.

When God is an angry dad, we think he's just waiting for us to mess up so he can discipline us. When we read, "Fear of the LORD lengthens one's life, but the years of the wicked are cut short" (Proverbs 10:27), we imagine God standing by to zap us whenever we lose our temper with the kids or let that cussword slip while driving in rush-hour traffic. In our moments of weakness, we expect to be met with shame and rebuke as our heavenly Father shakes his head with disappointment and marks a strike against us. We hear condemning voices in our head that say, "I told you so" and "When are you ever going to learn?" Our focus is to try very hard not to mess up so we don't risk exhausting the limits of God's grace and patience.

In contrast, when we think of God as a fairy godmother, we believe that if we do all the right things and follow a list of dos and don'ts, God will give us what we desire most in exchange for being good. We take pride in being good and right.

I'll give you a picture of this woman. She has a #Blessed T-shirt, coffee mug, and bumper sticker. She lives for the checklist and getting things done, but when hard seasons hit and unexpected brokenness comes, she is left spinning and questioning who she is and who God is. *Why would God allow this to happen to me if he loves me? I'm not as bad as that other lady at church, so God must be mad at me.*

Both the angry-dad and the fairy godmother views diminish the person and holiness of God. The angry-dad view robs God of his compassionate love and results in a fear-based obedience rooted in not making him angry or disappointed. Instead of providing a relationship marked by protection and care, the goal is to avoid punishment. The fairy godmother view reduces God to a "little g" god, someone we can manipulate and control based on our own efforts and devotion. Obedience is rooted in earning favor with God so he will give us what we want.

Fearing the Lord encompasses so much more than this. It means we not only approach God with humility but also make him the center of our lives. When we surrender ourselves to our good heavenly Father and run after him, we don't hide in a corner or live by a list of rules. Instead, we live as women who are free, knowing that God has our best interests at heart and that we aren't alone in either our failures or our victories.

Our aspirations are not merely to become "good humans" or to make sure that, on balance, we are more good than bad. There is so much more to life than that. We must set our sights higher. As we see in Proverbs 31, we can aspire to be strong, trustworthy, and wise women, not because we fear God's punishment or to complete our checklists, but because God is graciously working to make us more like him—for our good and his glory.

Our strength as women (and for all believers) is directly connected to our fear of the Lord. We live out an authentic fear of the Lord when we surrender to and trust in a holy and perfect God. Instead of our obedience being motivated by trepidation or earning favor, it is rooted in our love for and awe of God. His presence breathes encouragement and empowerment into our souls.

This is where every woman must begin her journey. Do you and I fear the Lord? Are we more concerned with his glory than our own? Do we surrender to what he has for our lives in both the good times and in the hard times? Do we take our walk with Jesus casually, or do we leverage all that we are to know him better? Being a biblical woman has a lot more to do with our surrender than it does with our talents and tasks. It has a lot more to do with being strong, immovable, and mighty for the Kingdom of God than it does with building our own kingdoms.

I love the promise of Proverbs 31:30: "A woman who fears the LORD will be greatly praised." The root of the Hebrew word translated "praised" is *halal,* which means "to shine." It is also the root of the word *hallelujah.*

The attributes of the Proverbs 31 woman are not a list of impossibly high standards, nor are they a job description for biblical womanhood. Instead, they describe what a person marked by wisdom—as personified by a woman—looks like. Wherever she goes, her very presence changes the atmosphere in the room—not because she demands attention or has to prove her worth, but simply because of who she is and how the light of God shines through her.

## Changing the Conversation from *Can't* to *How*

When I surrendered to God's call to ministry at age eighteen, I had no clue what that meant. I knew God was stirring in me, but I didn't know which path to walk down or even how to ask for directions. When I looked at examples of women in ministry, I didn't see many who were like me. I had started college with the dream of becoming a physical therapist, so I assumed God was directing me toward medical missions. Still, I felt a longing to study and teach God's Word, and to lead others on a similar path. I began to wrestle with God and to question what it meant for me to walk away from my own plans, and what it would look like for God to piece together my passions and desires with what he had planned for me. I tried to get some advice and wisdom from several pastors about what it meant to be called to ministry as a woman, but more often than not their replies included some form of the statement, "That's great that God is calling you to ministry, but just remember you can't _____."

What filled in the blank following *can't* would differ depending on who I was talking to and where they landed theologically on the issue of a woman's role in the church—a topic I hadn't yet fully studied for myself. Quickly feeling discouraged and isolated, I began to second-guess whether God knew what he was doing in stirring up all these passions in me for ministry.

You probably have your own list of phrases to fill in the blank following *can't*. Maybe you've even had a similar experience of excitedly sharing all that God was doing in your life, only to be met with caveats, concerns, and boxes you needed to work within.

What if we changed the conversation by focusing first on a celebration of who God made us to be? What if our starting point was the ways in which we are gifted and strong? What if we took encouragement from knowing that God has given each of us a unique story, personality, talents, and giftings to leverage for the Kingdom in any number of ways?

What if your confident and strong demeanor was celebrated as Deborah's was?

What if your desire to fill the gap and tend to hurting hearts was esteemed as Dorcas's was?

What if your ability to pore over Scripture was championed as Priscilla's was?

What if your faithfulness and sacrifice for the church was recognized as Phoebe's was?

What if you found yourself in a long lineage of faithful women, all of whom lived lives full of *cans* rather than *can'ts*?

When looking at the metanarrative of Scripture, there is so much to celebrate, and a lot can change in this conversation if we simply change the initial reply. Let's work to change the reply from *can't* to *how*.

How can God utilize your strengths to bring strength to structures and systems?

How can you take your deepest hurts and disappointments and turn them into offerings of worship?

How can your passions intersect with gaps and needs within your community?

How can developing your weaknesses and challenging some of your comforts expand your fear of the Lord and help you grow in new ways?

There are an infinite number of ways we can use *how* to live beyond the limits of *can't*.

Locking eyes with nine-year-old Langley on that Sunday morning when I stood at the front of the church reminded me of the only time during my childhood when there was a woman standing at the front of an old sanctuary waiting for me. It was Mrs. Blair, my counselor at a summer Bible camp. The preacher had asked all the counselors to come down front. I knew God was drawing me and that I needed to surrender my life to him. I caught eyes with Mrs. Blair, and she smiled at me, much like I had smiled at Langley. As a nine-year-old girl, I had also walked down the aisle to declare the most life-transforming decision a person could make. Mrs. Blair hugged me, and we talked through my decision to follow Jesus that day.

I hope Langley and the other girls and women in our church see someone like them when they come to church. I hope they see women who love Jesus with their whole hearts and leverage everything they are to serve, encourage, and share the good news of Jesus, because these are the marks of women who fear the Lord. I hope they see opportunities and pathways where they can use their giftings and personality to build up the church and expand God's Kingdom. And I hope you see these things too.

You may be at the very beginning of your leadership journey, or you may have decades of experience already under your belt. Regardless of the season in which you find yourself, I hope this book will not only reaffirm the need for your voice and gifts within your home, church, and community, but also reignite your passion to take your rightful place in the long line of faithful women who have been used by God to share his message of grace, love, and redemption.

In the pages that follow, we'll look with fresh eyes and eager hearts at some of the women in God's plan of redemption. As we dig into their stories, I hope you will find your own narrative wrapped up in the greater narrative of God's glory. But like any good story, we have to go back to the beginning to understand the author's original intent. So let's journey there together now, back to the opening pages of God's redemptive plan.

## DISCUSSION QUESTIONS

1. Who are some of the women in your life who showed you Jesus at a young age?

2. What messages did you receive about what it means to be a biblical woman? What misunderstandings were passed along?

3. What characteristics of the Proverbs 31 woman stand out to you, and why?

4. How do you respond to the idea that Proverbs 31 is not a checklist of requirements for biblical womanhood but a celebration of who women are? As you look at the Proverbs 31 woman, which attributes do you see in yourself?

5. What "Just remember you can't" messages have you received in your faith journey? What would it look like for you to walk out your giftings with a "How does God want to use me?" perspective?

## 2

# Made in His Image

**Hannah Anderson**

Deep Thinker | Author | Podcast Host

As a young twentysomething and a new mom, Hannah Anderson was trying to figure out what it meant to be a woman made in God's image. She wrestled with some of the ideas and concepts she'd been taught about biblical womanhood and gender roles—ideas and concepts that left her feeling inauthentic and frustrated.

"It wasn't until my daughter was about seven years old that things finally began to click for me," she said. "That's when I discovered I needed to find my identity not in my roles or my womanhood, but in God himself." This sent Hannah on a journey that ultimately led her to write her first book, *Made for More*.

Here's how Hannah described to me what she has discovered about being a woman made in God's image:

It seemed to me that we had spent a lot of time talking about what it meant to be a woman but not enough time talking about what it meant to be a person—what it meant to be an image bearer. And once you begin to ask and answer those questions, so much else makes sense. Once I understood that I had been made in God's image and that I was being redeemed and restored through Christ, the perfect image of God, everything else began to make sense too.

Women flourish by coming alive to God. I know that sounds a bit esoteric, but it's one thing to embrace certain categories of femininity, and it's another thing to know that God delights in your womanhood for its own sake—simply because he thought it was a good idea to make women and to make them in his image. There's a spiritual freedom that comes when you understand yourself this way.

This world is not made for women's holistic flourishing. Our society isn't, and too often neither is the church. This doesn't mean that we can't flourish but that we need to understand the source of the conflicts. We must be honest about the brokenness without becoming transfixed by it.

To do this, we must have a clear sense of who God says we are and keep that message central in our thinking. Sometimes this will mean pushing back against things that we all accept as normal by comparing our practices and traditions to the truth of Scripture. And sometimes it will mean making peace with the imperfections of our God-ordained context and working toward flourishing in all the ways that we can. At the end of the day, the goal is to move in the right direction in the right way. Things will never be perfect in this life. We will never be perfect in this life. But as image bearers, we have the promise that we're being made like Christ through it all—every relationship, every opportunity, every challenge is making us into the women God has created us to be.[1]

Hannah's words are wise counsel for all of us who are wrestling with the question, "Who am I?" Her answer is that we must first answer the question, "Who is God?" She redirects our attention back to the author's intent, the reason God created us in his image in the first place.

When we become women who first and foremost find our identity in God, we can then go out and reflect him in different ways as we serve, lead, rule, and work together with other image bearers to advance the Kingdom.

---

The first five minutes of a movie are pivotal. The opening scene, the first words and actions of the characters, the music that plays in the background and sets the mood for the story that will soon unfold. Numerous thematic elements all come together to spark emotions, pique interest, and draw viewers in for the next ninety minutes as a grand narrative unfolds.

That same dynamic is at play in the first words of the greatest story ever told. It is designed to leave us intrigued, informed, and leaning in for more.

## God's Intent and Purpose in Creation

"In the beginning God created the heavens and the earth" (Genesis 1:1).

These ten words kick off the grand metanarrative of Scripture. This is how things started. This is how planets came into motion. This is the beginning.

It makes sense for us to go back to the beginning to under-stand God's intent and purposes in why and how he created. Although some come to Genesis 1 and 2 looking for a scientific rundown of evidence—and there is truth there that speaks to science—this isn't the purpose for which the creation account was written. When Moses wrote these words for the nation of Israel and for us today, he wasn't concerned with scientific evidence so much as he was concerned with capturing the heart of God as Creator and his relationship with his creation, including his people.

Genesis 1 provides a bird's-eye view of the creation story. It establishes the cadence and rhythm of God's work in creation: There is an evening and a morning that mark the boundaries of each day. There are some elements of creation that build upon the others, testifying to God's order and purpose. For example, God creates the seas and land (Genesis 1:9-10) and then creates the ani-mals (Genesis 1:20-21, 24-25) that would inhabit them. Starting with the third day and ending with the sixth, the narrative includes the phrase, "God saw that it was good."

As God creates the creatures of the sea, the birds of the air, and the living creatures on land, Moses uses the phrase "of the same kind" to describe them. For example, "Their seeds produced plants and trees of the same kind" (Genesis 1:12). The Hebrew word translated "kind" here is *min*, which means "form and kind of species." *Min* is used ten times in verses 11-25. But when God describes human beings, he uses two new words: *image* and *like-ness*—"Then God said, "Let Us make man in Our image, accord-ing to Our likeness" (Genesis 1:26, NKJV). The Hebrew word translated "image" is *tselem*, which means "shape," "resemblance," or "shadow." In other words, our likeness is not to birds or fish or lions, but to God himself. The Hebrew word translated "likeness" is *demuth,* which means resemblance, model, and shape. Together, these two words demonstrate how humanity is distinct from other created things precisely because of our likeness to God. We are both a shadow and a reflection of who God is within the relationship (or communion) of the Trinity. Thus when God created human beings in his own image, and created us male and female (Genesis 1:27), he expressed the unity, diversity, and complexity of his own character as a relational, triune God. This is important in understanding both our need and our longing for God and for one another, and how as humans we are to relate to one another as fellow image bearers.

You may be thinking, *Why the Hebrew lesson?* or *Does it really matter?* It matters profoundly. Our purpose, our design, our very being is wrapped up intricately with God. We reflect his glory in who we are. The declaration that we are made in the image of God contains the first words spoken over and about human beings. It matters because it establishes the fundamental equality of men and women before God.

If we think of Genesis 1 as a canvas on which God begins to paint his creation with his goodness and likeness, then Genesis 2 is where he adds more color and texture to his masterpiece. We see this in several ways, beginning with a shift in the name used for God. In Genesis 1, God is *Elohim* (mighty one); in Genesis 2, starting at verse 4, God is also referred to as *Yahweh* (I am), and "Yahweh is the name commonly associated with the covenant relationship between deity and his people, Israel."[2] The use of *Yahweh* portrays a relational God who is intimate in the ways he works, speaks, and is present with his creation.

As God adds strokes of color to his masterpiece throughout the metanarrative of Scripture, he paints a picture of *us* and *with* by weaving in covenantal language. For example,

- When God reconfirms his covenant with Abraham, he states, "I will always be your God and the God of your descendants after you" (Genesis 17:7).
- When God tests Pharaoh with the plagues, he promises Israel, "I will claim you as my own people, and I will be your God" (Exodus 6:7).
- The prophet Zechariah declares God's promise to bring his people back to Jerusalem after exile: "They will be my people, and I will be faithful and just toward them as their God" (Zechariah 8:8).
- The author of Hebrews quotes the Old Testament prophet Jeremiah in affirming God's promise: "This is the new covenant I will make with my people on that day, says the LORD: I will put my laws in their hearts, and I will write them on their minds" (Hebrews 10:16).
- The apostle John writes, "Look, God's home is now among his people! He will live with them, and they will be his people. God himself will be with them" (Revelation 21:3).

There is a tenderness, possession, and identity in each brushstroke of our being. God isn't some far-off and distant deity who is watching as we wander and err; he is a close, purposeful, and intimate Creator who pursues us. That is the answer to the question of who God is, which means it is also the answer to the question of who *we* are, because we are his image bearers.

After going back to the beginning to understand who God is, we can ask the next question: Why did God create us? The answer to this second question gets to the heart of what it means to be image bearers as women.

## Woman as *Ezer*

Genesis 2 zooms in closer on God's purpose in creating man *and* woman: "It is not good for the man to be alone. I will make a helper who is just right for him" (Genesis 2:18).

When I think of a helper or helpmate, the image that first comes to mind is that of a sidekick or assistant—like Robin, Tinkerbell, or Dr. Watson. The helper holds the number two spot and rides shotgun, gives directions, and, if things get bad, steps in to save the hero from the evil villain. As a kid who grew up playing competitive sports, being the "helper" sounded like a perpetual second-place trophy. But that's not what "helper" means in Genesis 2.

The Hebrew word for "helper" or "helpmeet" is *ezer.* It first shows up in Genesis 2:18: "I will make a helper [*ezer*] who is just right for him." It's repeated again after Adam names the animals: "But still there was no helper [*ezer*] just right for him" (Genesis 2:20). There was distinction but no sameness when it came to the animals, and so they weren't suitable helpers. God's response isn't to make a different animal or another man from the dust, but to create a woman.

The word *ezer* is made up of two Hebrew roots: *'zr,* meaning to "rescue," "aid," or "save," and *gzr,* "to be strong." Are you thinking back to the description of the Proverbs 31 woman? I hope you are. *Ezer* is used twenty-one times in the Old Testament, primarily within a military and battle context, to convey the concepts of strength, savior, and rescuer. For example,

> O LORD, hear the cry of Judah
>     and bring them together as a people.
> Give them strength to defend their cause;
>     help [*ezer*] them against their enemies!

DEUTERONOMY 33:7

We put our hope in the LORD.
He is our help [*ezer*] and our shield.

PSALM 33:20

You are about to be destroyed, O Israel—
yes, by me, your only helper [*ezer*].

HOSEA 13:9

*Ezer* is used by God to describe himself within the covenant relationship. As an *ezer*, God will come alongside his people, protect them, act on their behalf, and fulfill his promises for his glory.

This suggests that the picture we should have of *ezer* in Genesis 2 is that the woman is built and fashioned by God to come alongside the man in strength and purpose.

In the New Testament, Jesus conveys something similar when speaking to his disciples before his ascension: "I will send you the Advocate—the Spirit of truth" (John 15:26). Some other translations use the word *Helper* instead of *Advocate*. This is how Jesus depicts the Holy Spirit's work in the life of a believer—as an advocate and a helper. In Trinitarian theology, no one says that the Holy Spirit is less than or weaker than God the Father; instead, all three members of the Trinity work in harmony with one another in perfect and holy communion.

In a similar way, women are created for God's purposes to work with and strengthen those we come alongside as we reflect the image of our Creator.

## The Same, Yet Different

In Genesis 2:21-24, God continues painting his Creation masterpiece as he fashions the woman. When reading or discussing the creation story, or even the characteristics of men and women in general, we tend to start with the differences. However, as we'll see in these verses, the creation account as a whole has a drumbeat of sameness and togetherness more than distinctness and separateness.

One distinction that should be noted is found in the words chosen to describe how God creates the man and the woman. With Adam, God is portrayed as something of a potter, who forms, molds, and shapes the dust of the ground into a man. In the description of God's creation of Eve, the text states that he "made" her by taking one of Adam's ribs (Genesis 2:22). The Hebrew word translated "made" is *banah*, which means "to fashion or build." So, whereas God molds and shapes Adam, he fashions and builds Eve. There is something distinct in how God makes the man and the woman.

Then God presents the woman to the man. Can you imagine his reaction and overwhelming joy? Up until this point, he has seen only creatures who are not like him—birds, fish, bears, gazelles—and then he sees *her*.

It makes me think of a groom on his wedding day. Yes, everyone wants to see the bride as the back doors of the sanctuary open, the music begins to play the bridal march, and she enters in her white dress. But then everyone in the room quickly looks back at the groom. Why? They want to see his response to her—his big smile of youthful joy and amazement, sometimes with tears rolling down his cheeks, and with a gaze that is set solely on *her*.

When Adam first sees his bride, he sings.

"At last!" the man exclaimed.

"This one is bone from my bone,
    and flesh from my flesh!
She will be called 'woman,'
    because she was taken from 'man.'"

GENESIS 2:23

The first recorded words of man are a song of celebration over woman. He doesn't sing a song of how different her body is or how her voice and hair are different. He doesn't sing about how he will serve her, the roles she will play, or who will do what tasks in the Garden. Rather, he sings about how she is the same. They are of the same substance. The same bone. The same flesh. And then the text summarizes this sameness with the phrase, "The two are united into one" (Genesis 2:24). They are together—with some beautiful distinctions, yes—but with a resounding hymn of togetherness.

Going back to the beginning, listening to God's original Creation song, gives us the answers to our questions about our identity and purpose. We were made by and for our Creator. That is our identity. We were made to sing his praises, to reflect his glory, and to mirror the community of the Trinity. That is our purpose.

We were made to be a reflection of God (Genesis 1:26).

We were made for dominion (Genesis 1:26).

We were made with distinction (Genesis 2:22).

We were made to "be fruitful and multiply" (Genesis 1:28).

We were made for companionship (Genesis 2:18, 23-24).

We were made as helpers, to lend our strength to others (Genesis 2:18).

## Who Needs Help?

We often try to define our identity based on factors outside of who we were created to be, whether it's what culture tells us woman-hood looks like or identity markers such as motherhood, work, or outer appearance. We can even find ourselves rooting our identity in another person, such as our spouse, our boss, or a parent. And yet when we go back to the opening scene of God's metanarrative and read the words of the divine screenwriter, we learn that we must build our identity and purpose on the foundation that was laid by him and him alone. The flesh on our bones, the blood pumping through our veins, the passion in our gut, the very breath we breathe—it all harks back to the value, dignity, and strength we bring to our world as women created in the image of God.

Whether single, married, or widowed, we were made to bring life, companionship, strength, and beauty to the planet. As teachers, politicians, doctors, homeschool moms, grocery store cashiers, and students, women step into many different kinds of environments and challenges and reflect the goodness of God.

The first time I taught about the role of women in redemptive history to the women in our church, we concluded with a table discussion about how this understanding of our identity and purpose might make a practical difference in our lives. I will never forget the response of one our most cherished older women, Mrs. Betty.

Mrs. Betty had lost her husband to brain cancer a few years earlier. As we began to talk about the meaning of the word *ezer* and being created in the image of God, she looked at me with tears puddling in her eyes and said, "I've been in church my entire life—six whole decades—and I have never heard these truths before. I always thought my role as a woman was to make sure things were tidy at home, and to let my husband make the big decisions. When he died, I felt like my purpose died too—that God was done with me."

Understanding our role in redemptive history—that to be an *ezer* is to be a source of strength—is a life-changing truth. And yet too often we set it aside and look to other things to give us a sense of worth and value.

We can easily say that God gives us our worth and defines who we are, but we get sucked into the lie that our life stages, accomplishments, or what we *do* defines us. Maybe you're single and, despite being told to be content in the waiting, you're frustrated and believe that you won't be complete until you settle down, find a spouse, and start a family. Or maybe you're a young mom devoted to shepherding your kids, but you find little fulfillment in wiping bottoms and picking up toys for the five-hundredth time in a day while your friends from college are traveling the world and living picturesque Instagram lives. Or maybe you're climbing the corporate ladder—staying late, answering the after-hours emails, and tidying up the loose ends, only to see your colleague get the promotion—and status—you were striving for. Or maybe you are like Mrs. Betty, struggling to build a new life after losing one of the most important pieces of your sense of identity and belonging.

New life stages, family, and work are all good things, but we can't allow them to become the central source of where we find our fulfillment, identity, and purpose. When we find our source of worth and value in external things, our identity and purpose die with them when expectations are unmet, change inevitably happens, and disappointment sets in.

But no matter what stage of life, vocation, or place on the planet we find ourselves in, being made as an *ezer* means that we look for ways to bring strength, truth, grace, and love to our situation. Whether in our teens or in retirement, in a bustling city or out in the countryside, in a house full of kids or an apartment with roommates, we reflect the image of God and the strength of his character.

We must persistently journey back to the Creation story and remember that our value, worth, and dignity come from God, who created us.

## Listening to the Voice of Our Creator

I have a beautiful group of women I get to live life alongside. We huddle around a dining room table every couple of weeks as ministers, nurses, a fitness coach, and moms. Some are extroverts, some introverts. Some of us are front-of-the-room leaders, and others function more behind-the-scenes. Our hobbies, traits, family backgrounds, and life stories are all different, and yet we share many of the same struggles, pressures, and questions. We sit around eating a homemade dessert and talk about life and God, and the two collide in different moments and seasons.

As we wrestle together with the realities of life, we often circle back to the issue of identity. We try to discern whether we are being true to ourselves and our purpose or trying to live up to someone else's expectations of who we're supposed to be. Maybe you have heard some of these same voices or felt these same expectations:

"You just need to find the balance."

"You don't know enough to speak into that issue or lead in that way."

"You should always have a tidy and clean home."

"You are too strong-willed."

"You need to lose just ten more pounds, and then you'll feel confident."

"You are too old for that."

"You don't have enough experience yet."

"You aren't smart enough."

"You're too emotional."

"You have to get that next degree or credential to stay on top."

"You have to juggle it all."

"You have to prove yourself first."

What if these voices and expectations were silenced by going back to the original question, "Who am I?" Especially when the answer is found not in something you're supposed to be, do, or accomplish, but in the inherent worth and dignity derived from your Creator.

You are an image bearer.

You are a co-ruler.

You are a strength-giver.

You are a protector.

You are a life-giver.

You are a reflection of a good, holy, intentional, purposeful, bringing-order-to-chaos, always-pursuing, and never-giving-up God.

Your every breath, every heartbeat, every gift and ability, every passion declares the glory of *who you are* in him.

## DISCUSSION QUESTIONS

1. What have you been taught about the creation of women? In what ways have those views been affirmed or challenged after reading this chapter?

2. In what ways have you seen women bring strength, provision, protection, and help to various situations? How have you done the same?

3. What voices have caused you to doubt your identity and gifts? How have you seen God pursue and form you uniquely to reflect his glory?

4. What voice of expectation are you aware of as a woman at your current stage or season of life? How does the truth of God's purposeful creation of women help to combat those expectations?

5. In what areas of your life have you tried to seek your identity and purpose instead of first finding it in God? Describe a time when one of those areas caused frustration or failure and how those moments pointed to a need to realign your heart.

# 3

# Women and Singleness

**Lina Abujamra**

Physician | Speaker | Humanitarian

Lina Abujamra grew up in Lebanon during a time of civil war. To escape the war, she moved to Chicago at the age of fifteen. As a teenager, she experienced God's presence in a profound way and surrendered her life to whatever God would have for her.

She ended up studying medicine at the Medical College of Wisconsin and became a pediatric emergency room doctor at Edward Hospital in the Chicago suburbs. God used her there to be a light and voice of hope for her patients. When a young teen girl was admitted to the hospital after trying to hang herself, Lina looked tenderly into the young girl's eyes and whispered, "God has a plan for your life."

God has not only used Lina to impact the lives of countless young people and their families in the Chicago area, but
also many in her home country. In 2013, as the civil war in Syria
escalated and refugees poured over the border into neighboring Lebanon, God stirred Lina to share the hope of the gospel in
her native land. She gathered her team and set up two traveling
medical clinics to assist with humanitarian needs and share the
gospel with those who were suffering in much the same way she
had as a young girl.

In addition to practicing medicine, Lina hosts *Today's Single
Christian* on Moody Radio and is the founder of Living with
Power Ministries. She writes, speaks, teaches, and connects
biblical answers to the questions of everyday life. One of the big
questions she has had to wrestle with personally is remaining
single after breaking off two engagements. In her book *Thrive:
The Single Life as God Intended*, she offers encouragement for
other singles:

> Your purpose as a single Christian is to please the Lord.
> You cannot please the Lord when you're nursing a grudge
> about your singleness. You cannot please the Lord when
> you're questioning His judgment and criticizing His will.
> You cannot please the Lord when you place your desires
> higher than His purposes for your life.
>
> Your purpose in life has not been botched by your
> singleness. You are not a mutant in God's design for
> marriage. God created you for the sole purpose of
> knowing Him and making Him known. Your singleness is
> God's perfect place for you to thrive. You don't have to
> wait for your knight in shining armor to start living. You
> can know the Lord fully and serve Him wholly right here,
> right now.[1]

Whether sharing hope with her patients behind the curtain in an ER or with groups of women while onstage proclaiming God's faithfulness, Lina exemplifies a life fully surrendered and free in the hands of a good Father.

---

This may date me a bit, but when I was growing up in Texas, the hopping place to be was the local roller-skating rink. This was especially true in the blazing-hot summer months. Unless you were outside in a pool, there wasn't much else you could do to survive the sweltering temps, so Josey Skateland was the place to be. It had freshly waxed hardwood floors, a large disco ball sending sparkles across the room, and the best nineties hip-hop music blaring from the speakers.

I had these sweet white Rollerblades with lime green and pink trim that I got for my birthday one summer, and I loved nothing more than to strap them on over my white tube socks and glide into the circular flow of skating traffic with all the confidence and charisma in the world. Round and round my friends and I would go, talking about life and singing our hearts out to "Ice Ice Baby." Vanilla Ice was a local superstar after all. But there was one moment during every skate session that I both dreaded and was mesmerized by—the couples skate.

The deep-throated voice of the DJ resonated through the overhead speakers: "Could we get all of our couples, young and old, on the rink for our couples skate?" Those of us who were not paired off reluctantly left the wooden rink and grabbed our spot at one of the outlying tables. Then we watched all the teenage couples make their way around the rink hand in hand, looking googly-eyed and smiling brightly. Nine times out of ten, the DJ played a Boyz II Men song as he lowered the lights, cued the fog machine, and turned the lively skating rink into a heavenly paradise as the couples glided on clouds. The rest of us watched, secretly hoping that at least one of the guys would accidently trip and give us some comic relief.

I hated the couples skate because I was missing valuable skate time. I remember thinking it was so unfair that we had to just sit back and watch. The couples didn't want to skate anyway! They would have been just as happy sitting at a table and staring at one another. But as I said, couples skate also mesmerized me. There was something magical about it, and I hoped one day I would have someone to circle the rink with, hand in hand.

That experience of being single at a couples skate is one that bears some similarities to what it's like to navigate ministry, leadership, and life for a single woman today. Traditional evangelical culture places a premium on marriage. You haven't arrived or aren't credible until you are married with two and a half kids, a dog, and a mortgage. Women's ministries and conference messages directed to women often assume that those present are wives and mothers, never giving mention or notice to those who are single in the audience.

Too often, highly qualified, gifted, trained, and talented single women are overlooked and left on the sidelines of the church while married women (and men) use their gifts to serve and lead. And yet when we look at Scripture, we find that some of the most prominent women in Jesus' life and ministry were single. Among them were Mary Magdalene and Mary and Martha of Bethany.

## Mary Magdalene

Eager to learn, faithful to follow Jesus wherever he went, and pure in her desire to cling to Jesus when life was hard, Mary Magdalene is a supreme example of what it means to follow Jesus.

Soon afterward Jesus began a tour of the nearby towns and villages, preaching and announcing the Good News about the Kingdom of God. He took his twelve disciples with him, along with some women who had been cured of evil spirits and diseases. Among them were Mary Magdalene, from whom he had cast out seven demons.

LUKE 8:1-2

When Jesus freed Mary from those seven demons, she devoted her life to following him.

All four Gospel accounts acknowledge Mary as being present at the empty tomb and among the women who were the first to proclaim the resurrection of Jesus to the disciples. John's account also records a special encounter between Mary and the resurrected Jesus.

She turned to leave and saw someone standing there. It was Jesus, but she didn't recognize him. "Dear woman, why are you crying?" Jesus asked her. "Who are you looking for?"

She thought he was the gardener. "Sir," she said, "if you have taken him away, tell me where you have put him, and I will go and get him."

"Mary!" Jesus said.

She turned to him and cried out, "Rabboni!" (which is Hebrew for "Teacher").

"Don't cling to me," Jesus said, "for I haven't yet ascended to the Father. But go find my brothers and tell them, 'I am ascending to my Father and your Father, to my God and your God.'"

> Mary Magdalene found the disciples and told them,
> "I have seen the Lord!" Then she gave them his message.
> JOHN 20:14-18

This passage portrays a beautiful and intimate exchange between Jesus and a woman he had healed, who then walked alongside him throughout his ministry. They had no doubt laughed together, shared tears of mourning together, and felt the sting of death together.

One of the things that strikes me most about Mary Magdalene is her sold-out commitment to her Savior. He freed her from a life of torment and oppression, and her wholehearted response was to live out her freedom by following her Savior. Throughout the Gospel accounts, she is noted as a woman who faithfully remained with Jesus as he and his disciples traveled from town to town. She may have also provided financial support (see Luke 8:1-3).

Her Savior became her life, even in his death.

## Mary and Martha of Bethany

Among Jesus' closest friends were the sisters Mary and Martha and their brother, Lazarus. The Gospels make no mention of either sister being married. Luke records that when Jesus traveled to Jerusalem, "Martha welcomed him into her home" (Luke 10:38). It's easy to read that line and think nothing of it, but the fact that Jesus would enter the home of a woman shows his desire to affirm the worth and dignity of women at the time.

The Greek word translated "welcomed" in Luke 10:38 is *hypo-dechomai*, which means to welcome someone under one's roof. It is used only three other times in the New Testament—when Zacchaeus welcomed Jesus, when Jason welcomed Paul and Silas, and when the writer of Hebrews describes the Old Testament prostitute Rahab, who welcomed the Jewish spies. Again, we might read these descriptions and think nothing of what they did. But each of these acts of hospitality required taking a personal risk.

- Zacchaeus risked embarrassment and humiliation when he climbed the sycamore tree to catch a glimpse of Jesus, who was passing by. As a tax collector, he risked further derision and judgment when he joyfully welcomed Jesus into his home (Luke 19:1-10).
- Jason welcomed Paul and Silas by providing shelter and protection when they arrived in Thessalonica. When a mob stirred up trouble looking for Paul and Silas, Jason's home was attacked. He was accused of treason and thrown in jail (Acts 17:5-9).
- Rahab welcomed the Jewish spies even though it meant risking her life. Despite the dangers, she rejected the false god of her people, hid the spies, and directed them to safety (Joshua 2, Hebrews 11:31).

Hospitality is always about the good and protection of the one being welcomed, and Martha expressed this posture of a welcoming and sacrificial heart in her devotion to Jesus. Welcoming him was about so much more than making sure the lamb didn't burn and the table was set. Martha used her resources, time, and position to minister to Jesus.

Mary of Bethany, Martha's sister, is famously known for sitting at the Lord's feet while her sister was preoccupied with meal preparations. Jesus' response to Mary is another indicator of his desire to include women in his ministry. Throughout Jesus' visit with the two sisters, he disregards the cultural norms of the day to invite not only two women, but two *single* women, into the mission and ministry of God.

Shortly before Jesus' crucifixion, it is Mary who seizes an opportunity to minister to Jesus.

> Mary took a twelve-ounce jar of expensive perfume made from essence of nard, and she anointed Jesus' feet with it, wiping his feet with her hair. The house was filled with the fragrance.
>
> JOHN 12:3

Both her actions and her posture display humility, awe, love, sacrifice, and devotion. Here is a single woman who freely lavishes a prized and expensive possession, equivalent to a year's wages (John 12:5), as an act of worship. She gives it all away to Jesus. At a time and in a culture that made little provision for single women, Mary surrenders what was considered a source of security, provision, and worth to show Jesus, and those watching, just how priceless he truly is.

We read in the following verses that Judas opposed this act of sacrifice, characterizing Mary's generosity as both wasteful and careless. A gift equivalent to around three hundred denarii (a year's wages) would later be contrasted to the measly thirty pieces of silver that Judas received in exchange for betraying Jesus. Don't miss the contrast John is making. A single woman who is humble and abounding in sacrificial love is portrayed in stark contrast to a greedy, self-righteous man.

Mary Magdalene and Mary and Martha of Bethany were single women who feature prominently in the life and ministry of Jesus. They each contributed their own giftedness, worth, and devotion as they followed Jesus. They were faithful women who left everything to follow their Savior.

These women no doubt felt the sting and frustration of being single in a society that attached greater value and worth to marriage and having children to carry on the family name. Today, more than two thousand years later, single women continue to experience similar struggles. And while motherhood and marriage are good blessings from God, they are not the only avenues in which women reflect the glory of God.

## Singleness as a Gift

In his first letter to the Christians at Corinth, the apostle Paul includes singleness among the gifts God gives: "I wish everyone were single, just as I am. Yet each person has a special gift from God, of one kind or another" (1 Corinthians 7:7). Paul also notes the advantages of being a single woman: "A woman who is no longer married or has never been married can be devoted to the Lord and holy in body and in spirit. But a married woman has to think about her earthly responsibilities and how to please her husband" (1 Corinthians 7:34). If the apostle Paul, and Jesus for that matter, embodied the best of what it means to be single while living their lives for the Kingdom, how could we consider singleness anything less than the gift Paul says it is?

When I think about the single women I know who live for the Kingdom, I am always impressed with how resilient, strong, and sacrificial they are. My friends Allison and Gretchen are two examples. These twin sisters put down roots in their college town after graduation and are now well into their careers. After working long days at demanding jobs in education and mortgage lending, respectively, they are nevertheless among the first to show up for Wednesday-night Bible study. On Sunday mornings, they open the church doors and greet members and visitors arriving for the early service, and they regularly volunteer in the children's ministry. Simply put, our church would be severely lacking without them. They are free to serve, and they choose to give all that they are to those around them.

But here's an important thing to know about Allison and Gretchen: They are able to contribute their gifts because a married woman in the church already made them feel welcome and part of a larger family by saying to them one Sunday morning, "Come and sit with me."

Every person experiences loneliness from time to time, but for singles, being lonely can also create a unique challenge to fight for joy and to trust in God's sovereignty. The companionship of fellow believers is an answer to that longing for community, and it is a reminder of God's grace. When singles have a medical need, there are those in the family of God who can check in and make meals. When singles struggle with contentment and trust, members of the church family can come alongside to listen, pray, and point to the hope of our future Kingdom. When singles face an unexpected job loss, the church family is there to help pay the electric bill and network for new opportunities.

Sadly, however, singles are oftentimes overlooked or marginalized in the church and left to feel unvalued, underutilized, and un-thought-of. When I asked a group of singles about the common messages they hear at church, they responded with statements like these:

"There's something wrong with you if you're single."

"It's your fault you're single. You are too picky. You need to lower your standards."

"If only you were content, God would bring someone into your life."

"You are not a full-fledged adult until you're married."

"There is nothing here for you to do until you're married."

Yet when we read in the Gospels about how Jesus treated single women, we find such contrasting messages:

*Learn from me.*
*Walk with me.*
*Eat with me.*
*Cry with me.*
*Live for me.*

I recently asked a single friend who is in her late thirties this question: What is the one thing you wish you heard more from the church about singleness?

"Well, first," she said, "there is one thing I would love to *never* hear again. I don't want to be told how I just need to be patient and wait for my Boaz. To be honest, at this point I'm not sure that's what God has for me. But what I would *love* to hear is that my church sees me and celebrates my service, and that they are with me on this journey."

I looked at her with a smile and said, "Let's go celebrate you."

## DISCUSSION QUESTIONS

1. *How does the devotion of Mary and Martha of Bethany and Mary Magdalene challenge you in your own willingness to lay down your preferences and plans to follow Jesus?*

2. *Biblical hospitality is an attribute we see throughout Scripture—that we as believers are to welcome and care for the physical and spiritual needs of others. How does this contrast with what cultural hospitality looks like?*

3. *In what ways have you seen the church marginalize singles? If you are married, what are some practical ways you might include singles in your own life? If you are single, what would you like*

*your married friends to know about how you'd like to be included
or invited in?*

4. *If you are single, how have you seen your fellow single friends
display servanthood, sacrifice, and faithfulness? If you are
married, what have you learned from the service, sacrifice, and
faithfulness of your single friends? What are some ways you can
foster and encourage them?*

5. *Think about the prominence of single women in the daily
ministry of Jesus. How can the church come alongside single
women and widows to better include them in both the family and
mission of God?*

## 4

# Women and Marriage

**Betty Howard Elliot**

Bible Translator | Missionary | Teacher | Author

Betty Howard was born to a missionary family in Brussels, Belgium, in 1926. A few months later, the Howards moved to Pennsylvania, where Elisabeth would grow up with four brothers and a sister. Betty was introverted but also sharp and determined. While a student at Wheaton College, she studied Greek in hopes of later translating the Bible into the languages of undiscovered people groups throughout the world. At Wheaton, she met a young man named Jim, who seemed to hold just as much fervor, passion, and dedication for the spread of the gospel as she did.

Although they had deep feelings for each other, both Betty and Jim wondered whether God was calling them to single-ness so they could fully pursue their individual callings. After ministering separately for five years, they saw God bring them to a place where they could serve alongside one another. On October 8, 1953, Betty became Mrs. Jim Elliot, whom many today know as Elisabeth Elliot. Less than two years later, on February 27, 1955, their daughter, Valerie, was born. Now living as missionaries in the jungle of Ecuador, the Elliots loved their God and one another deeply. They also loved the people in their midst who had never heard the gospel.

Tragedy struck less than a year later, on January 8, 1956, when Jim and four other missionaries were speared to death as they attempted to make contact with a tribe called the Waodani. The love story that had started with such passion and devotion ended in agony and sorrow.

When many thought she would return home, Elisabeth continued to minister and serve the people of Ecuador for several years. Through God's gracious plan, she ended up being welcomed by and living among the Waodani tribe who had killed her beloved husband. She watched God transform her deep pain and loss into the redemption of a people group whom many said would never hear the gospel.

Eventually she chose to move back to the United States and used her gifts as an author, a teacher, and a radio-program host. She met Addison Leitch, a professor of theology at Gordon-Conwell Theological Seminary in Massachusetts, and they married in 1969. Sadly, another loss would come far too soon when Addison died after a battle with cancer less than five years later.

In 1977, Elisabeth married a hospital chaplain named Lars Gren, and they were married until her death at age eighty-nine on June 15, 2015, after suffering ill health and dementia for many years.

In her posthumously published book, *Suffering Is Never for Nothing*, Elisabeth wrote these beautiful words to encourage others who have suffered deeply:

There have been some hard things in my life, of course, as there have been in yours, and I cannot say to you, I know exactly what you're going through. But I can say that I know the One who knows. And I've come to see that it's through the deepest suffering that God has taught me the deepest lessons. And if we'll trust Him for it, we can come through to the unshakable assurance that He's in charge. He has a loving purpose. And He can transform something terrible into something wonderful. Suffering is never for nothing.[1]

⚬

After attending the University of Texas at Dallas for two years, I transferred to a small Bible school called Criswell College. I knew nothing about the school other than that my pastor at the time was a professor of preaching there. I wanted to know and teach the Bible like he did, and I was eager to dive into this thing called theology and equally excited to make some Christian friends along the way.

I told God two things before walking through the double doors to Herschel Hall for new-student orientation. The first was, "God, I am yours. I trust you with whatever your calling and plan is for my life." The second was, "I will never marry a preacher."

God often uses the "I will never" statements to show us that he has a bigger plan in mind, but that morning I thought I had a pretty good plan of my own if he would just go along with it. Of course, it was in that orientation that I got a first glimpse of Josh King, who is now my husband. And yes, he became a pastor, which means I am now a pastor's wife. Was it love at first sight? Nope. In fact, we laugh to this day about how much of an unconventional start we had. But it was on that day that God began writing a story in two young twentysomethings about what it means to trust him and to choose a covenant life together.

Our vow was, "No out, just through," meaning we wouldn't try to escape the challenges we might face as a couple but find a way to persevere and grow through them—together. Divorce was not an option. By God's grace, he has carried us through seasons of both flourishing and hardship.

As I look back on the tension I felt in laying down my fears of what it meant to be a pastor's wife and how I thought it would require setting aside God's call on my life, I not only see how inaccurate my view of marriage was but also how inaccurate my picture of God was.

Marriage has a lot less to do with gender roles and finding a spouse who completes you than it does with a daily sanctification and pursuit of love that is embodied by selflessness, goodness, and grace. Author and pastor Tim Keller puts it this way:

> When over the years someone has seen you at your
> worst, and knows you with all your strengths and
> flaws, yet commits him- or herself to you wholly, it is a
> consummate experience. To be loved but not known is
> comforting but superficial. To be known and not loved
> is our greatest fear. But to be fully known and truly
> loved is, well, a lot like being loved by God. It is what we
> need more than anything. It liberates us from pretense,
> humbles us out of our self-righteousness, and fortifies us
> for any difficulty life can throw at us.[2]

Marriage is a mirror for God to reflect, move, and chisel out his character in a bride and a groom as they show faithfulness, forgiveness, and love.

What I thought was going to be the end of my individual calling ended up being a shared partnership in which my husband's weaknesses met my strengths, and my strengths met his weaknesses. Not a perfect match by any means, but two willing hearts.

## The Church as the Bride of Christ

When we think of a bride, we think of her white dress and beautiful hair and makeup, and the anticipation of her walking down an aisle to her groom while surrounded by family and friends. Weddings, at least in Western culture, are considered the "bride's day," and it's helpful to use that as a lens when we consider that the church is the bride of Christ. Jesus is so enthralled by the beauty of his bride, the church, that he can't wait for her to walk the aisle, join him, and live together with him happily ever after.

Although there is no doubt that Jesus sees his people, the church, as full of beauty and distinction, the relationship has much more to do with Jesus' love for the bride than it does with anything the bride can give or do or be for the groom. In fact, when the Old Testament describes God's people as the bride, the bride is a prostitute. The story of Gomer and Hosea provides a compelling analogy as we try to make sense of Jesus' love for the church.

Hosea, a prophet and man of God, is told by God himself to marry a prostitute named Gomer. Even after their marriage and despite Hosea's unfailing love for Gomer, Gomer runs back to her familiar life of prostitution. Despite her unfaithfulness, Hosea pursues his wife, buys her back, and forgives her. Hosea is a picture of Jesus. Jesus would leave glory to come and pursue, love, and ultimately sacrifice himself for the good and redemption of God's people, who nevertheless treated his love as expendable and cheap.

They followed him and became mesmerized by the miraculous things he could do for them, but when it came time to follow him to the Cross, even those closest to him left.

When we think of marriage, instead of thinking of a wedding, we need to think first of the gospel, the good news for the undeserving and broken bride. The gospel isn't so much about the people who make up the church as it is about Jesus' love and pursuit of the people he came to redeem and make whole.

So when we think about marriage by first thinking about the gospel, we make a series of exchanges. In exchange for expectations of what we think a godly wife should be, we focus on the root of the gospel, which is love. This is both freeing and empowering. In exchange for expecting perfection, we view marriage as a process and a journey. In exchange for living out separate roles, we work toward mutual goals and seek to foster one another's flourishing. When we begin with the gospel, even a disagreement becomes an opportunity to choose one another again and to pursue intimacy. When love is the focus, each new stage of life is a chance to build trust, experience sanctification, and allow the gospel to transform our own soul and the soul of our spouse.

If the gospel is the mark of a marriage and a wife is both the giver and recipient of that good news, then being a wife is primarily about who you are becoming rather than whichever role you're playing. The gender roles, financial and home responsibilities, and decision-making all have more to do with who you and your husband are *together* than what you do individually. Apart from the gospel, we are lost, dying, and scraping to bring life to dry bones; but in the gospel, we breathe, change, and move toward holiness because of the work of the Spirit within us.

Marriage is a context in which our brokenness and flaws are intertwined with love, intimacy, togetherness, and vulnerability.

The result is a beautiful mirroring of the oneness of the Trinity as husband and wife serve together and grow stronger in the Lord together. Two women in Scripture, Sarah in the Old Testament and Priscilla in the New Testament, provide compelling examples of what it looks like when God's redemptive purposes are lived out this way in the context of marriage.

## Sarah

What first comes to mind when you think of Sarah in the Old Testament? Maybe you think about how she was so beautiful that her husband told her to lie—twice—so he wouldn't be killed. Maybe you think of the mean woman who created a plan to have a son through her maidservant, Hagar, and then mistreated her so badly that she ran away—and then, years later, cast her out for good. Or maybe you recall how she laughed at God when she was told at the age of ninety that she would have her first child.

Sarah is a character whose story is full of twists and turns and ups and downs, but also lessons of faith and trust in even the most unthinkable circumstances. The transparent telling of her flawed story within the pages of Genesis shows us that as we journey through different seasons of disappointment, fear, and waiting, God is at work in our struggles.

When Sarah and her husband, Abraham, are first mentioned in the Bible, her name is Sarai, and his is Abram. When God called Abram to leave his family and his land—the only life he had ever known—Sarai was right beside him (Genesis 12:1-6). If you or I were to do something like that—to leave everything behind and begin traveling with no idea where we were going or what we would do when we got there—our friends and loved ones would probably consider it a crazy idea at best. They'd encourage us to choose a destination, make a plan, count the cost, and, ideally, have a job waiting for us. And yet Abram and Sarai stepped out in faith and followed God into the unknown.

Even though Sarai was a woman of courage and faith, she was also marked by doubt and insecurity. I'm so grateful that God, in his grace, shows us real women in Scripture who are trying to wrestle through what it means to be a faithful follower of Yahweh while still being 100 percent human and flawed. After ten years of not conceiving the child God had promised her, Sarai devised her own plan to have a child (Genesis 16). She gave Hagar, her Egyptian slave, to Abram to build a family. After Hagar became pregnant, the two women were at odds with one another, and Sarai was so mean to Hagar that Hagar ran away (Genesis 16:6).

And yet when God offered to make a covenant with Abram, both he and his wife were also given new names. Abram became Abraham, and Sarai became Sarah (Genesis 17). Despite her barrenness, disappointment, and misguided actions, God met her with blessing, faithfulness, and a new name. God exchanged Sarai, the name that represented her old life, home, and barrenness, for Sarah, which means "princess" or "kings of peoples shall be of her."

God chose Abraham and Sarah to be a part of his redemptive story despite what they could offer him or how well they would follow him. When Sarah privately laughed to herself upon overhearing the Lord tell Abraham that she would have a child in her advanced age, the Lord heard and acknowledged her disbelief. He knew the deepest parts of her heart, even the parts she voiced to no one but herself. He didn't reprimand her or tell her how lacking in faith she was but instead re-centered her heart on the one who had made the promise: "Is anything too hard for the LORD?" he asked (Genesis 18:14).

Sarah's story reminds us that even when we have a limited view of ourselves and our circumstances, God is bigger and holds the answers to our hearts' questions and desires. When we are tempted to become bitter and close ourselves off to the wonder of who God is, or when we scoff at what we think can't be done, God is still listening and remains eager to speak to us and answer us. As Sarah eventually trusted the Lord to fulfill his promises, she was transformed from a jealous and barren woman into a woman who joyously mothered a child from whom would come a nation vaster than the stars in the sky and the sand on the seashore.

We are like Sarah whenever we step out in faith and trust God with what we don't know about the future. And we are also like her when we try to take control and manipulate and outwit our circumstances for more immediate results.

Sarah shows up again in the New Testament when the writer of Hebrews presents a list of faith "Hall of Famers":

> It was by faith that even Sarah was able to have a child, though she was barren and was too old. She believed that God would keep his promise. And so a whole nation came from this one man who was as good as dead—a nation with so many people that, like the stars in the sky and the sand on the seashore, there is no way to count them.
>
> HEBREWS 11:11-12

Sarah wasn't remembered for her doubt or her mean mistreatment of another; she was remembered for her faith. It's significant that Sarah is recognized in her own right rather than paired with her husband's faith. In Hebrews 11:8-10, Abraham is applauded for his obedience and faith, and then Sarah is celebrated for her own story of obedience and faith.

Abraham and Sarah are examples of what so often happens within a marriage when the two individuals bring their strengths, weaknesses, insecurities, and doubts to God and one another. They believe that God will birth trust, obedience, and sacrifice—first in relation to God and then in relation to each other. One is not lost in the other, but both walk alongside each other in complementarity and togetherness.

## Priscilla

Priscilla is a woman in the New Testament who embodies what it means to serve the church and God's Kingdom with wisdom, strength, and faithfulness. She was a wife and a ministry partner who was anchored deeply in the theology of God's Word.

Priscilla and her husband, Aquila, are first mentioned in Acts 18 as partners with Paul in their joint profession of tentmaking. They were also ministry co-laborers with Paul in Corinth and sailed with him to both Syria and Ephesus (Acts 18:18, 24-26). It is in Ephesus that Priscilla meets Apollos, when she and Aquila hear him preaching in the synagogue. Although Apollos is described as "an eloquent speaker who knew the Scriptures well" (Acts 18:24), his knowledge of the gospel was incomplete. And so Priscilla and Aquila "took him aside and explained the way of God even more accurately" (Acts 18:26).

The Greek word translated "explained" is *ektithēmi*, which means to expound or to declare. The same word is used later in Acts when Paul "explained [*ektithēmi*] and testified about the Kingdom of God and tried to persuade them about Jesus from the Scriptures" (Acts 28:23).

What a beautiful picture this is of discipleship and pouring one's life, knowledge, and example into another. Priscilla's role in the life of Apollos helps us to see that women are to know, understand, and pass on to others God's truths. Alongside her husband, she taught, explained, and declared the narrative of Scripture. Apollos eventually went on to help proclaim the gospel of Jesus to the Jews.

## Encouragement for Wives from the Epistles

In addition to the examples of Sarah and Priscilla, several women mentioned in the New Testament epistles stand as sources of encouragement and wisdom for wives. Just as the attributes of the Proverbs 31 wife are a means of celebrating women, I believe the examples of these New Testament women can be a means of championing who a wife is to be instead of what she is supposed to accomplish.

The ways that Paul and Peter describe the actions and attributes of these women are instructive. They speak to the character of every woman who is molded and shaped by the Spirit of God, which is the end goal for all women and believers. Here are examples from three passages:

**Titus 2:4-5**
Training younger women
Wise living
Purity
Doing good
Submitting to husbands

**1 Peter 3:1-4**
Submitting to husbands
Purity and reverence
Known for beautiful character instead of outward appearance
Gentleness and peacefulness

1 Timothy 3:11
Respectability
Not slandering
Self-controlled
Trustworthy

These characteristics aren't things we can merely *will* ourselves into being, but instead are the fruits of a woman transformed over time when she is chosen, adopted, and called by God.

I definitely had to grow into these characteristics as a young wife. When Josh and I married, he was twenty-three and I was twenty-one, and I thought we were exactly the same. We were both strong, stubborn communicators with hearts for the church. I thought our similarities meant we were set for a pretty easy road ahead.

The easy road lasted all of one week and officially ended when we went to buy groceries after returning home from our honeymoon. We had a huge fight in the deli section about whether to buy generic cheese or Kraft. I'm sure the other shoppers at Walmart thought we had lost our minds. My naivete of thinking our similarities would keep us from disagreement was on full display.

Even so, it was the first of many fights that taught us how to bring our passions, similarities, and distinctions together to show honor, love, and appreciation for the other. When we both ate our sandwiches the next day, it meant far more that we were eating together than it did what kind of cheese was between the lettuce and the turkey.

## DISCUSSION QUESTIONS

1. How does the picture of two people's strengths and weaknesses coming together help us to understand how togetherness is more effective than working apart?

2. From the list of characteristics that describe how a wife (and really all women in Christ) should be identified, which attributes stick out most to you, and why?

3. How does focusing on the relationship of Christ and the church help frame your understanding of marriage?

4. In what ways has your understanding of marriage or roles within marriage been affirmed or challenged by what you have read in this chapter?

5. How do the differences in our personalities, passions, and giftings help us to reflect the image of God in marriage?

## 5

# Women and Motherhood

**Kristen Williams**

High School Teacher | Mom to Five Girls | Adoption Advocate

"Hi. I'm Kristen. I'm a single high school teacher from Cincinnati, Ohio. I'm so excited to meet you all, and I'm praying that God allows me to adopt a little girl." These were the first words I read from a woman who was then a stranger, but whom I now get to call friend, fellow adoptive mom, and sister.

Kristen says, "I always knew I was supposed to be a mom. I never found a person with whom I could commit in marriage, but as I got older, I began exploring adoption because the desire for motherhood never diminished. I prayed for months before finally taking that first step of faith."

Kristen and I were both pursuing overseas adoptions, and we kept up with each other's journeys as we completed mountains of paperwork, court documents, and physical and psychological wellness checks. As she got closer to adopting a child from India, I asked her what was drawing her to adopt from that country. She shared how she wanted to extend love and protection to young girls who were often considered expendable, valueless, and burdensome.

Kristen's match with her first daughter, Munni, was marked by both joy and deep sorrow. As she read Munni's paperwork and saw the physical scars on her face and scalp, she knew Munni had suffered abuse in a culture that too often devalued girls. Kristen says, "When I saw her face in the photo, it was like an electric current shot out and hit me in my heart. She was everything I wasn't looking for, and she ended up being everything I needed." On Valentine's Day 2013, Kristen officially became Munni's mother.

Six months later, Kristen adopted another young girl from India—three-year-old Durga, who had been abandoned at birth. Like Munni, she had been rejected by those who were supposed to love and care for her. She then experienced multiple rejections from prospective adoptive families because her physical appearance bore the scars of abuse. Durga had been found in a garbage pile, barely clinging to life. Her nose and part of her upper lip had been eaten away by animals and insects. When Kristen and Munni welcomed Durga to their family, they gave her a new name: "Roopa," which means "blessed with beauty."

Kristen has continued to grow her family through adoption and now has five beautiful daughters: Munni, Roopa, Mohini, Sonali, and Snigdha.

When reflecting on what motherhood has taught her about God, Kristen shares that it is wrapped up in the word *refinement*.

For me, becoming a mom and parenting my daughters has revealed my sin and selfishness like nothing else.

Every single day, I see new selfish tendencies and worldly desires in myself. God has tenderly led me through this refining fire. It burns, but what he brings forth from it has been incredible growth and a deep intimacy with him. Through this journey, I have learned of his faithfulness and unconditional love—not merely as reciting words I've memorized, but of knowing in the deepest places of my heart and spirit that he will never ever leave me.

Understanding the love I have for my daughters has also increased my comprehension of God's fatherly love for me. Prior to becoming a mom, I only understood his fatherly love from the perspective of being his child. But being a mother and knowing how much I love my girls—how I would do anything for them, how my heart hurts when theirs does, how I want to protect them and guide them—has amplified my understanding of God's love for me.

This dear friend is a picture of resilience, compassion, and grace—the very definition of a mother who loves as God loves his own.

---

In God's grace, he gives us friends to walk with in different seasons of life. And sometimes he gives us friends who are faithful and steady throughout multiple seasons of life—through moves, job losses, and the changes that come with each new phase of adulthood. Beth Hallock is one of those friends for me. Although we grew up in the same city and played against each other in the same softball league, we didn't really form a friendship until we were both in our newlywed season of life. She is quirky, has the best one-liners, is an introvert, and hates conflict. Although we are exact opposites in a lot of ways, we found each other while serving alongside students at the same church. With her witty humor and my need for a partner in ministry, we instantly hit it off.

Beth's mom was diagnosed with ovarian cancer when Beth was just nine years old. After an up-and-down battle through chemo and radiation, her mom died when Beth was sixteen. When most of her peers were getting their driver's licenses and picking out dresses for the homecoming dance, Beth was trying to navigate becoming a woman without the most important woman in her life. For her, motherhood was associated with death rather than life. Motherhood became even more complicated after she was married and experienced infertility. Month after month, she hoped God would bless her and Jeremy with a viable pregnancy, only to have her hopes crushed by disappointment and loss.

Year after year, I watched her navigate her sadness on Mother's Day. When I asked her how she managed it, she said, "Mother's Day had always been the lowest and worst day of the year because I didn't have a mom. Then it became absolutely intolerable when all I wanted was to be a mom but couldn't. Every year that gut-punch got bigger. My friends knew I wouldn't be available. I had no interest in going to church, where everyone was happy and celebrating with their moms. Instead, I would crawl into a hole and hide until Monday."

I understood some of Beth's sadness more deeply when Mother's Day came around after I had suffered a miscarriage at nine weeks. It shifted my entire perspective of what it means to be a mother. I realized that motherhood isn't limited to things like changing a child's diapers and teaching the ABCs. It includes providing a sense of belonging, nurturing, and protection—gifts that are expressed and fostered differently across the scope of motherhood. Like Eve, the first mother, women are uniquely created to reflect the image of God in this treasured role, with all its joys and sorrows.

## Hannah's Prayers

The book of 1 Samuel begins with the story of a man named Elkanah and his two wives, Hannah and Peninnah. The drama in the story begins with a bit of rivalry: "Peninnah had children, but Hannah did not" (1 Samuel 1:2). Peninnah taunted and mistreated Hannah due to her inability to conceive (1 Samuel 1:6). It's not hard to imagine that in a culture where a woman's worth was equated with her ability to have children, Hannah experienced the sting of rejection, longing, and brokenness.

When I think of Hannah, I see the faces of the many women I know who hold the pain and loss of motherhood. Whether it's a woman who can't conceive, a birth mother who selflessly places her child for adoption, or a foster mother who steps into loss and brokenness, so many women find camaraderie and solace with Hannah.

The text says, "Hannah was in deep anguish, crying bitterly as she prayed to the LORD" (1 Samuel 1:10). The Hebrew phrase literally means "bitterness of soul." Hannah was angry, bitter, questioning, longing, and grieving. The weight of her suffering was so heavy that the priest Eli, who was watching Hannah as she prayed, thought she was drunk. For the deepest of griefs and losses, there are no words that provide comfort—only a slew of emotions and questions that take the form of tears and physical heaviness. Perhaps you've felt this deep bitterness of the soul in your own life.

Holly felt it month after month, year after year, as she and her husband prayed and tried to conceive a baby and start a family. The hopes and prayers that intertwined between calculating dates and showing up at doctor appointments led only to a series of disappointments.

Nadia felt it when she and her husband chose to adopt two brothers from the foster care system who had faced neglect, drug abuse, and other traumas. The sacrifice and readjustments of opening their family of five to two more created a tight squeeze in a 1,700-square-foot home, but that was easy compared to shepherding the boys through soul wounds that seemed incapable of healing.

Stacey felt it when what was supposed to be routine lab work for her fourteen-year-old son came back with a leukemia diagnosis just before the Christmas season. Days that were supposed to be celebrated with family enjoying presents and games around the table were reluctantly replaced with doctor appointments, chemotherapy, and watching her once-vibrant son fight to keep down liquids.

The tears, questions, anguish, and loss women across the planet feel today are emotions Hannah knew well. The helplessness, lack of control, and supplications of the waiting seasons were etched into her life. And yet in her deepest dismay, she approached God in humility and trust and found respite in prayer. She prayed, "If you will look upon my sorrow and answer my prayer and give me a son, then I will give him back to you" (1 Samuel 1:11).

Hannah acknowledged that God is the ultimate giver of life, and in a profound act of sacrificial love, she offered to give back to God the one thing that only God could give her. She would give what she received back to the Giver. What a beautiful picture of motherhood! That is the blessing every woman can give— to embrace the blessings God gives and then openhandedly offer them back to God in sacrificial gratitude. Even in our losses and our longings, this is how we allow God to be the ultimate guide of our own hearts and the hearts of those we nurture and shepherd.

The happy news for Hannah was that God blessed her with a son, whom she named Samuel. Hannah kept her vow—after the boy was weaned, she said, "I asked the LORD to give me this boy, and he has granted my request. Now I am giving him to the LORD, and he will belong to the LORD his whole life" (1 Samuel 1:27-28). We not only see God's grace in answering Hannah's request but also Hannah's example of obedience, trust, humility, commitment, and character—both before and after God answered her request.

After surrendering Samuel back to God, Hannah made a beautiful declaration of her joy in the Lord and praised his attributes (1 Samuel 2:1-10). Here is a summary of some of those traits:

- He is strength.
- He is rescuer.
- He is holy.
- He is unmatched.
- He is judge.
- He is in control of both life and death.
- He is the giver of wealth.
- He is for the needy and marginalized.
- He is order.
- He is protector.
- He is all-powerful.

Hannah could have easily held her son, God's answer to her prayers, with tight fists. Instead, she opened her hands and offered the best gift she had ever received back to the Giver. Whether or not we are mothers, the lesson we learn from Hannah is that our opportunity as women is to steward both the unanswered longings and the answered prayers as sacrifices to the Lord. God is the ultimate giver of every gift, and we can honor him in the waiting and the wrestling as well as in the answers. When we do, we experience meaning, identity, belonging, and purpose.

## Mary, the Mother of Jesus

If you had to make a list of qualifications for a woman who would become the mother of God, what would be on your list? Would she need to be of a certain age or socioeconomic class? Would she need to look a certain way? Come from a certain family? Be able to quote certain passages from the Torah? What an intimidating job list for any woman!

In the grace of God, he looked down and saw a young virgin girl from a lower-class family who was living in an insignificant city named Nazareth, then chose her to be the mother of the most influential man the planet has ever known. Here is the first description we have of Mary:

> In the sixth month of Elizabeth's pregnancy, God sent
> the angel Gabriel to Nazareth, a village in Galilee, to a
> virgin named Mary. She was engaged to be married to a
> man named Joseph, a descendant of King David. Gabriel
> appeared to her and said, "Greetings, favored woman!
> The Lord is with you!"
>
> LUKE 1:26-28

When I hear the word *favored*, I automatically think of *favorite*, as in, God chose Mary because he loved her more than any other young girl at the time. But that is not what *favored* means here. The Greek word is *charitoō*, which means "to pursue with grace, compass with favor; and to honor with blessings." In this case, understanding what it means to be favored isn't so much about knowing the qualifications of Mary as it is knowing the grace of

God in choosing Mary to begin with. The verb *charitoō* is related to the noun *charis*, which is often translated as *grace* in English. I can't think of a more needed descriptor and motivator in motherhood than the need for grace and the giving of grace.

Paul uses both *charis* and *charitoō* in his letter to the church at Ephesus: "We praise God for the glorious grace [*charis*] he has poured out [*charitoō*] on us who belong to his dear Son" (Ephesians 1:6). This grace is not only modeled and shown in the life of Mary but is also what you and I get to experience as women who are likewise called, redeemed, and sealed by the work of Jesus Christ.

So it isn't that Mary checked off items on some list of qualifications or accomplishments; instead, in God's goodness, he chose to impart his grace and blessing to a young, unlikely, and probably overlooked girl.

But still, Mary faced an unusual human reality: On an otherwise ordinary day, an angel named Gabriel appeared and announced that she would have a child, even though she hadn't been intimate with a man. None of this was on her agenda for the day. Can you imagine the shock and confusion she must have felt?

And yet, after this huge drop of life-changing news, Mary asked only one question: "But how can this happen? I am a virgin" (Luke 1:34). She was trying to put the pieces together, trying to make sense of this amazing news. In response to her one gentle question, Gabriel laid out some pretty heavy theology: "The Holy Spirit will come upon you, and the power of the Most High will overshadow you. So the baby to be born will be holy, and he will be called the Son of God" (Luke 1:35).

Do you see the glimpse of the Trinity in Gabriel's answer? He acknowledged God ("Most High"), "the Son of God," and "the Holy Spirit." In this declaration, we see the beauty and togetherness of God the Father, the Son, and the Spirit, all of whom were at work with grace, favor, and tenderness in God's redemptive story—in the life of a woman.

Mary's response? "I am the Lord's servant. May everything you have said about me come true" (Luke 1:38). She did not complain, bargain, or negotiate. There was no "Have you run this by my parents?" or "Could I check with my fiancé and get back to you in the morning?" She offered no excuses, nor did she name other women who were more qualified than she was.

Consider what a contrast her response is to that of Moses, one of the heroes of the Old Testament. When God himself appeared to Moses in a burning bush and told him he would lead the Israelites out of slavery to the Egyptians, the reluctant prophet was full of rebuttals and excuses: "Who am I to appear before Pharaoh? Who am I to lead the people of Israel out of Egypt? . . . What if they won't believe me or listen to me? . . . I'm not very good with words" (Exodus 3:11; 4:1, 10). It takes approximately twenty-five verses of dialogue for Moses to accept his new role and mission from God—a stark contrast to Mary's simple and humble, "I am the Lord's servant."

## Marked by Surrender

When I consider the stories of Hannah and Mary, both of them mothers of sons whom God used to lead the nation of Israel and ultimately the Kingdom of God, I'm struck by their willingness to trust God and surrender their beloved children to him.

As both judge and priest, Samuel became the godly leader and prophetic voice Israel needed. He was a pillar to the nation in its transition to a kingdom, and he stood as a messenger between its first two kings—Saul and David—and the Lord. Because Hannah surrendered her son, Samuel lived his life for God and the people of God.

Jesus became the Savior who turned the world and religious systems of the day upside down. He healed the lame, proclaimed repentance, fed the hungry, and sat with the outcast. His mother, Mary, followed in his steps as he poured out his life. She was with him even as he made the journey to Calvary. She saw her beloved son unjustly beaten, stripped, and crucified. When Mary surrendered her son, he also lived his life for God and the people of God.

Similar to Hannah, Mary also had a song of praise for the Lord. Look closely at the parallels between their two songs:

| Hannah's Song (1 Samuel 2:1-10) | Mary's Song (Luke 1:46-55) |
|---|---|
| [1] My heart rejoices in the LORD! The LORD has made me strong. Now I have an answer for my enemies; I rejoice because you rescued me. | [46] Oh, how my soul praises the Lord. [47] How my spirit rejoices in God my Savior! |
| [2] No one is holy like the LORD! There is no one besides you; there is no Rock like our God. | [49] For the Mighty One is holy, and he has done great things for me. |
| [4] The bow of the mighty is now broken, and those who stumbled are now strong. | [50] He shows mercy from generation to generation to all who fear him. [51] His mighty arm has done tremendous things! |
| [5] Those who were well fed are now starving, and those who were starving are now full. | [53] He has filled the hungry with good things and sent the rich away with empty hands. |
| [9] He will protect his faithful ones, but the wicked will disappear in darkness. No one will succeed by strength alone. [10] Those who fight against the LORD will be shattered. He thunders against them from heaven; the LORD judges throughout the earth. He gives power to his king; he increases the strength of his anointed one. | [54] He has helped his servant Israel and remembered to be merciful. [55] For he made this promise to our ancestors, to Abraham and his children forever. |

Seeing these two songs side by side demonstrates a bridging of generations, Testaments, and the lineage of grace.

God is actively working and moving in our surrender. Hannah and Mary received the grace and wisdom they needed to train up their children in the law of the Lord, but they also needed that same grace and wisdom to trust God in the letting go.

## Spiritual Mothers

Many New Testament writers use familial language for the church, which I love! When they speak of making disciples, they speak of our need for one another in the context of a great big—and sometimes dysfunctional—family. Within this family, older women are to pour into, invest in, teach, and shepherd younger women—something God calls all women to do whether or not they have biological ties. And the need for spiritual aunts, grandmothers, and big sisters within the church today is more pressing than ever.

In his letter to Titus, the apostle Paul wrote,

Teach the older women to live in a way that honors God. They must not slander others or be heavy drinkers. Instead, they should teach others what is good. These older women must train the younger women to love their husbands and their children, to live wisely and be pure, to work in their homes, to do good, and to be submissive to their husbands. Then they will not bring shame on the word of God.

TITUS 2:3-5

As noted previously, singleness is in no way a disqualifier for being a woman who pours wisdom, godliness, and goodness into another—which means that this passage applies equally to all women, not just to those who are married or have children. In fact, such pouring into others is exactly what women were made to do, and the church provides the avenues and spaces for such mentoring relationships.

As a woman who has served other women, from girls' ministry through women's ministry, I have seen what a gift the members of the body of Christ can be to one another. Whether it's a young woman taking a teenage girl under her wing, a widow walking a friend through a midlife divorce, or an empty nester listening over coffee to an exhausted young mom of three, the power of community is an essential source of wisdom and strength for women walking through seasons of darkness. Spiritual motherhood is a call for all women to live grace-filled, sacrificial, surrendered lives for the good of others.

## DISCUSSION QUESTIONS

1. *Who is a woman in your life who has modeled motherhood for you? What have you learned from her in both positive and negative ways?*

2. *What stands out most to you when comparing the songs of Hannah and Mary? What key attributes of women are evident in their words? How do these attributes compare with what our society encourages women, and moms, to be?*

3. *God used a season of waiting in Hannah's life and humble beginnings in Mary's life to display his power. In what ways does this encourage you in your own struggles or limitations? What do you think it means in practical terms to surrender hard parts of your story so that God can use them for his glory?*

4. *We all have a call to come alongside other women and influence, inspire, and pour into their lives. Share any experiences you have had of being mentored by another woman in the faith, or of mentoring someone yourself. What did you learn about the significance of being a spiritual mother?*

# 6

# Women and Work

**Zim Ugochukwu Flores**

World Traveler | Entrepreneur | Author

Zim Flores grew up in a single-parent household with a strong Nigerian mom, Uchenna, who initially came to the US for an arranged marriage but then fled to California with her two children when her husband became abusive. After various moves, the three moved back to Minnesota for a time and then ended up in North Carolina. Early on, Zim learned how to adapt not only to the relocations but also to being the only African in her communities. Her adaptability birthed a passion to build, create, and thrive.

Zim's résumé speaks of her natural abilities and giftedness and includes such achievements as cloning a gene as a freshman in college and becoming the youngest election-precinct judge in North Carolina. Zim's passions and drive enabled her to accomplish more in young adulthood than many others might accomplish in a lifetime. In 2011, while still a senior in college, she was recognized as one of *Glamour* magazine's "20 Amazing Young Women Who Are Already Changing the World."[1]

After college, Zim moved to India for a year as a Henry Luce Scholar, and it was in this season that she launched Travel Noire, a boutique travel company so successful that it landed Zim on the *Forbes* "30 Under 30" list in 2016.[2] She and her company also received recognition from *Black Enterprise* magazine ("25 Black Women Who Are Changing the World") and *Fast Company* ("Most Innovative Companies in the World").[3] Oprah Winfrey celebrated Zim's achievements by selecting her as one of the "SuperSoul100."[4]

After years of hustle, hard work, and dedication, Zim felt God leading her to let it all go. In 2017, she sold Travel Noire and found herself in a season of pruning and refining as she separated her identity, value, and worth from her work and career. It was a time of darkness and questioning during which she wrote a book, called *Dare to Bloom*, about what it meant to fully trust God with her surrender. In an interview, Zim stated,

> I hope that those who read the book can be reminded that our identity is always safe with God. Even when the world tells us that we are this kind of person or that kind of person, we have sixty-six books that tell us the kind of person we are. We are made in the image of God. We are his image-bearers. He has put something very special within all of us. And if we only knew how special we were and we are, I think that, that would make the process of starting over so much easier for a lot of people.[5]

Zim has since launched several new businesses, one being Italicist, an online tech company that uses computer-vision technology to help women discover modest clothing. Zim says, "Change doesn't start with planting; it begins with uprooting."[6] Her story of surrendering her gifts, talents, and ultimately her life challenges us to chase after the story God is writing in us, because it is worth far more than any story we could write ourselves. Trust him to write your new beginning.[7]

---

The Women's Bureau of the US Department of Labor, which celebrated its one hundredth anniversary in 2020, recently published a study that tracks the most common occupations for women by decade over the last one hundred years. The data shows that in 1920, more than 8.1 million women were in the workforce, and the top three jobs they held were domestic- and personal-service workers, teachers, and stenographers/typists. By 2019, the number of women in the workforce had skyrocketed to more than 79.4 million, with the top three professions being teaching, nursing, and nursing/psychiatric/home-health aides.[8] Various factors play into the rising numbers and professional shifts over each decade, but it is clear even in just a one hundred–year span that women are a vital part of the flourishing, health, and productivity of a society.

From the beginning of Scripture to the end, work is portrayed as part of what it means to reflect the image of God. In our creativity and in our ruling and managing of resources, we fulfill God's call to Adam and Eve: "Be fruitful and multiply. Fill the earth and govern it. Reign over the fish in the sea, the birds in the sky, and all the animals that scurry along the ground" (Genesis 1:28). Adam and Eve together were to rule the earth. In the Creation story, God worked for six days and then rested on the seventh. Work existed before the Fall, and God deemed it good. But if work was part of Eden before the Fall, why does the issue of work seem to be such a point of tension and pressure for women today?

Depending on the values of your family of origin, your cultural context, and your faith tradition, you likely have some thoughts and expectations about what you believe a woman should or shouldn't do in regard to work. You may have been taught that working outside of the home is sinful and stealing from your family. You may have grown up in a home where you were told to make your own career path and not rely on a spouse or handouts. The perspectives on what's ideal range from the 1950s stay-at-home mom to the contemporary "leaning in" corporate executive.

Between both ideals, there are gifted, talented, and capable women who want their lives to matter and whose circumstances hardly fit into a simple equation of when to work or not work. So it's helpful to exchange the question, "Should women work?" for a broader question: "Why women and work?" In exploring that question, we discover that women have been part of God's work from the beginning of time, and their contributions have been made in both the home and the marketplace. Two excellent examples of working women in Scripture are Ruth in the Old Testament and Lydia in the New Testament.

## Ruth

Recently widowed, Ruth committed herself to her mother-in-law, Naomi, who was also a widow. Her now famous vow to Naomi was, "Wherever you go, I will go; wherever you live, I will live. Your people will be my people, and your God will be my God" (Ruth 1:16). Together, the two women left Moab, Ruth's home country, and traveled to Naomi's hometown of Bethlehem. For

Ruth, this meant moving to a land that wasn't hers—a land with a different culture and a different God. And yet Ruth proved herself steady, hardworking, and faithful.

Part of the Mosaic law stated that farmers were to leave behind portions of their crops for gleaners, the poor and marginalized who owned no land and could not grow their own food. It was a gracious way to provide for those who had nothing. However, this provision was not a handout; it required hard work to gather the leftover crops. As a gleaner, Ruth no doubt spent long hours on her hands and knees gathering enough grain to sustain her and Naomi.

She could easily have left to go back to her home country.

She could easily have gathered only enough for herself to eat.

She could easily have bailed on her vow to Naomi and pursued a new husband.

She could easily have stolen from people she didn't know.

But she didn't.

She was faithful.

She was hardworking.

She was patient.

She was submissive.

She was humble.

And it so happened that she did the hard and faithful work of gleaning in the field of a man named Boaz. When Boaz learned of Ruth's story and saw these attributes in her, he generously provided for Ruth and Naomi and ultimately became the kinsman-redeemer of her story.

When Ruth humbly and gently asked Boaz to marry her, he responded, "I will do what is necessary, for everyone in town knows you are a virtuous woman" (Ruth 3:11). The Hebrew word translated as "virtuous" is *khayil*. It appears 246 times in the Old Testament and usually conveys the idea of strength and valor in a soldier. Much as soldiers defend their posts, keep watch, protect their fellow soldiers, and fight for their people, Ruth was an *ezer* woman who came alongside her mother-in-law with a faithful, protective, and brave love. She was *khayil.*

Ruth's worthy character is also acknowledged in the New Testament when her name appears in the genealogy of Jesus (Matthew 1). Boaz and Ruth were the great-grandparents of King David, and all three are included in the lineage of Jesus, the Savior of the world.

Ruth's vow to Naomi is the vow I repeated to Josh on our wedding day. It is a beautiful reflection of the faithfulness and loyalty God shows to those who are his children. As we reflect his character and heart in the world, the work we do brings expressions of his goodness, faithfulness, and provision to a broken planet.

## Lydia

At the start of his second missionary journey, the apostle Paul had a vision that sent him to Macedonia (Acts 16:9-10). On the way, he stopped in the city of Philippi, where he stayed several days. As he usually did on the Sabbath, Paul went looking for other believers in this new city. As he walked the riverbank, he approached a group of women who had gathered, and among them was Lydia (Acts 16:13-15).

Lydia was from Thyatira, a colony of Macedonia that was a melting pot for those of various nationalities and religious backgrounds. Although the main god there was Apollo, there were a small number of Jewish believers who were part of the local synagogue. The city also boasted several trade guilds in which artisans were trained and then perfected their craft, such as cloth dyeing, metalworking, and leatherworking. These artisans were the creative entrepreneurs of the day, minus the Etsy storefronts and flat shipping rates.

Thyatira was a hub of commerce and business, and Lydia was right in the middle of it all. She is described as "a merchant of expensive purple cloth" (Acts 16:14). According to Bible scholar Herbert Lockyer, "The water of the area was so well-adapted for dyeing, that no other place could produce the scarlet cloth out of which fezzes were so brilliantly and so permanently dyed. This unique purple dye brought the city universal renown."[9]

To put Lydia in modern-day terms, I imagine her as the woman at New York Fashion Week with her hair slicked back, wearing oversized glasses, and rocking high heels as if they were her house slippers. She rubs shoulders with the prominent. Kate Middleton would be pictured on the front cover of a fashion magazine in one of Lydia's original creations. L.Y.D.I.A. would be trending on Instagram. Okay, maybe the Instagram thing goes too far, but this was a woman who hustled, traveled to the big city, and made a brand for herself. And little did she know the work God was going to do in her life on her day off, when she would hear Paul preach at the riverside. Acts 16:14-15 says, "The Lord opened her heart, and she accepted what Paul was saying. She and her household were baptized."

Don't miss the fact that as Lydia and the other women were observing a religious ritual by gathering for prayer, they were still missing the message of Jesus. In Paul's sharing of the gospel, we see the Lord's pursuit and grace in opening Lydia's heart. Her immediate step of obedience was to be baptized. Much as the cloth she labored over was saturated in dye, she, too, was drenched by the waters of baptism and made beautifully new in Christ.

After she and her household were baptized, Lydia invited Paul and his ministry partner, Silas, into her home. Don't miss the significance of the fact that it was *her* household and *her* home—her wealth, stability, and independence were remarkable for a woman at that time. Lydia leveraged everything she had to serve others. I love it that when she invited Paul and Silas to her home, she refused to take no for an answer. The text says, "She urged us until we agreed" (Acts 16:15). This was a strong and accomplished woman who argued with the apostle Paul and won.

When Paul and Silas later landed in jail, God sent an earthquake to free them of their shackles. Knowing he would be executed if his prisoners escaped, the Roman jailer was about to take his own life when Paul and Silas intervened and ended up leading the jailer and his household to Christ. The next day, when Paul and Silas were released from prison, can you guess where they went? To Lydia's house, and "there they met with the believers and encouraged them once more" (Acts 16:40). Lydia's house was both a haven for Paul and Silas and a gathering place for believers.

The Greek word translated as "encouraged" in Acts 16:40 is *parakaleō,* meaning to "comfort," "console," "call to one's side," or "implore." Does this word and imagery ring a bell? Think back to the truths we covered in chapter 2 about Eve being created from Adam's side as a helper, comforter, and friend.

In the story of Paul and Silas's release from prison, we see the two missionaries comfort and encourage the believers at Lydia's house. We can also infer that Lydia—by using her resources to care for Paul and Silas during their stay—encouraged them as well.

## Work as an Offering

In his first letter to the church at Corinth, the apostle Paul wrote, "Whether you eat or drink, or whatever you do, do it all for the glory of God" (1 Corinthians 10:31). The Greek word translated "do" is *poieo,* which means to "produce," or "make," or to "spend your time." For most of us moms, *doing* takes the form of the work we undertake to care for and support our families.

The context of Paul's message concerns food and idolatry. He charged the Corinthians not to repeat the sins of the Israelites who pursued lives of pleasure and chased meaningless created things rather than living for their Creator. However, the same charge applies to us today in the context of our work. We are not to use our work merely to accumulate wealth, power, or achievement, but instead we are to use our talents, smarts, abilities, and creativity as an offering to our Creator. The talents and gifts he gives us are to be used for him. When we lay down our work as an offering, God uses our time and our efforts for the good of others and to reflect his glory.

If you are a stay-at-home mom of young children and feel lost in the monotony of changing diapers and trying to figure out what your child is screaming about for the hundredth time in a day, know that God is using your sacrifice and care to reflect his infinite care for your child.

If you are a corporate executive who feels the constant pressure of maintaining profitability and leading your staff as you champion them to flourish in their own God-given abilities, you, too, reflect the shepherding heart of the Father.

When given as an offering, the work of the homeschooling mom, the grocery store cashier, and the woman on Wall Street all have equal honor, value, and dignity—not because of what each woman produces but because of the one for whom she produces it—her Creator.

## Work as a Context for the Gospel

Our work often allows us to rub shoulders with people who have a whole array of ideologies, backgrounds, ethnicities, and viewpoints. Conversations at the coffeepot can range from politics to kids' sporting events to a new recipe you tried the night before—and all of those conversations can be opportunities to point others toward the gospel. In the workplace, we can be light in the darkness as we reflect the characteristics of God to our coworkers. As women of integrity, truth, diligence, and patience, we exemplify Spirit-filled lives rather than lives driven by the flesh. Whether we're debating cultural ideals or discussing how to ethically meet sales quotas, our witness speaks to those around us about the need for a Savior.

In addition to providing a context in which to share and live out the gospel, work is also an environment in which God teaches us and refines our character. When things get hard or we aren't sure we're going to achieve our goals, pushing through our fear of failure produces perseverance. When we get tired of dealing with the same stubborn and cantankerous personalities (or maybe we are that stubborn personality) but still treat others with respect, we learn what it means to have patience and how to be long-suffering. When coworkers or friends get promotions or accolades for jobs well done, we learn what it means to have joy even when feeling passed over. Our willingness to follow the lead of our bosses over our own thoughts and plans nurtures both self-control and humility. Work is a school in which the Holy Spirit teaches us how to be more like our Father and how to advance his Kingdom instead of building our own kingdoms.

Work is a gift from God. As women, our work is a gift to the world. Whether you're managing endless spreadsheets, raising a child, running an inner-city after-school program, or painting a canvas, you can do it all for the glory of God.

## DISCUSSION QUESTIONS

1. How would you characterize your daily work? How does knowing that God made us to create and build help to influence your contentment in the work you have?

2. Do you view work as a burden—something that **must be** done? How does viewing your work in light of who God is and how he has uniquely gifted you change your perspective of your work?

3. In what ways has your work helped to sanctify you and make you more like Christ? What is something recently that God has used in your work to encourage your heart to be more like his?

4. How can you fight against finding your identity first in the work that you do instead of in how God has made you and his definition of identity?

5. What opportunities does your daily work provide for you to both be the gospel and share the gospel?

# 7

# Women and Mission

## Karen Watson

Corrections Officer | Missionary | Martyr

Karen Watson was a thirty-eight-year-old woman who worked as a corrections officer for her local sheriff's department. She went through a difficult season when three people close to her—her fiancé, her grandmother, and her father—all died within a two-year span. After a time of searching and questioning, she discovered the truth and grace of the gospel, and her life was transformed. She found new hope and had a desire to share the message of Christ with everyone around her.

After taking a few short-term mission trips, Karen applied to the International Mission Board to serve overseas in Iraq. Iraq had just been invaded in what would be the first stage of an ongoing war, leaving many people displaced and without water, homes, or protection. In 2003, Karen flew to Iraq to join a team of other American missionaries to help build a water purification system and to aid refugee women. God had equipped her with gifts and abilities to serve and had transformed her life story. Now she was able to share that story with many who were walking through their own deep grief and loss.

Tragically, Karen's life was cut short. On March 15, 2004, attackers with AK-47s shot at a van carrying Karen and several of her friends, killing her and three others.

Before leaving for Iraq, Karen had given her pastor a letter to be opened only in the event of her death. Dated March 7, 2003, it read,

*Dear Pastor Phil and Pastor Roger,*

*You should only be opening this in the event of death.*

*When God calls there are no regrets. I tried to share my heart with you as much as possible, my heart for the nations. I wasn't called to a place; I was called to Him. To obey was my objective, to suffer was expected, His glory my reward, His glory my reward . . .*

*The missionary heart:*

- *Cares more than some think is wise*
- *Risks more than some think is safe*
- *Dreams more than some think is practical*
- *Expects more than some think is possible.*

*I was called not to comfort or to success but to obedience. . . .*

*There is no Joy outside of knowing Jesus and serving Him. I love you two and my church family.*

*In His care,*
*Salaam, Karen*[1]

Karen's heart for hurting people took its last beats on earth the day she died, but her words, obedience, and faithfulness became the heartbeat behind God's continued work for years to come. Her example has changed the lives of many people. Some were inspired to surrender their lives to work for God in foreign missions, some planted churches because of her story, and many others came to faith at her funeral.

The only material possessions Karen left on this earth were her Bible, her journal, and her duffel bag, but her legacy of devotion lives on, and her story continues to be told as men and women follow in her footsteps of surrender. She now lives in God's glory, her reward.

———————— ◉ ————————

As a young girl, I attended a program at my church called Girls in Action. Each week, we studied different missionaries from all over the world and learned about their lives and their ministries. For a young girl from Texas, it was a window into a whole new world. The cultures and stories intrigued me, but the missionary life also seemed like a calling that just wasn't mine. That was for "them" and others who *really* loved Jesus.

When I surrendered to ministry as a freshman in college, I immediately recalled what I had learned all those years ago about the families who had sold everything to go to Africa, China, and the ends of the earth. *Is this what God is calling me to do?* Ultimately I understood that God was calling me to short-term missions. I would still study premed and become a physical therapist. I would take those skills to Africa from time to time and then come home to my first-world luxuries.

Over time, God graciously showed me that being on mission was for every believer, not just the ones who chose to leave their hometowns. All of us who are redeemed and changed by Jesus are called to a mission. And he eventually did ask for my obedience to pack up and leave home for a foreign land (otherwise known as Arkansas) where they call queso "cheese dip."

There is no way to be a follower of Jesus and *not* be on mission. Everything about his life and his calling for us to lay down our lives and follow means that we are living for a mission bigger than ourselves. Jesus is about his Kingdom and getting that message of the Kingdom to the ends of the earth—to the streets of your town, the hallways of your schools, the corridors of your offices, the homes of your neighbors, and beyond. God is a missional and moving God, and we are the means by which he shares his message.

Two examples of biblical women who knew what it meant to be on mission are the Samaritan "woman at the well" and the women who were the first to proclaim Jesus' resurrection. These women shared the gospel with confidence and joy.

## The Woman at the Well

The Gospel of John records the well-known story of a conversation between Jesus and a Samaritan woman, who is also referred to as "the woman at the well." Jesus does some pretty remarkable things in this story, some of which were taboo at the time. For starters, he traveled through Samaria on a route not typically traveled by Jews, who despised Samaritans. Then he speaks with a woman, which was unheard of for rabbis. And she is not just any woman, but a woman with such a bad reputation that she avoids all the other women in town by choosing to draw water from the well in the heat of the day rather than the cool morning hours. In spite of the fact that Jesus is tired and thirsty, he treats her with grace, truth, and understanding.

The Samaritan woman is understandably shocked and confused and tries to figure out why Jesus would even engage her in conversation. The text says, "The woman was surprised, for Jews refuse to have anything to do with Samaritans. She said to Jesus, 'You are a Jew, and I am a Samaritan woman. Why are you asking me for a drink?'" (John 4:9).

In his book *The Gospel according to John*, New Testament scholar D. A. Carson explains the history behind the woman's question:

> After the Assyrians captured Samaria [the capital of the northern kingdom of Israel] in 722–721 BC, they deported all the Israelites of substance and settled the land with foreigners, who intermarried with the surviving Israelites and adhered to some form of their ancient religion (2 Ki. 17–18). After the exile [of the southern kingdom to Babylon], Jews returning to their homeland . . . viewed the Samaritans not only as the children of political rebels but as racial half-breeds whose religion was tainted by various unacceptable elements. . . . About 400 BC the Samaritans erected a rival temple on Mount Gerizim.[2]

As a Samaritan, the woman at the well knew she was considered an unclean, impure, half-breed, heretical follower of God. And yet Jesus chose to sit with her and converse with her. Ultimately, he also put her on mission, using her to proclaim his message.

Sister, as you read this book, I have no doubt there are things you believe disqualify you from doing the work of God. Maybe it is the untold secret of an abortion. Although you know that God has forgiven you, you still walk in the shame and regret of that decision, and you deeply believe God could never really use you for his glory. Or maybe it is the sting of abuse and the lies Satan whispers to you that you aren't loved. Much like the Samaritan woman, you were used and then left to pick up the pieces. Whatever ugliness and hardships our stories may hold, this story gives us a picture of a weary and thirsty Jesus who loves to come alongside women and offer living water that never runs dry.

We learn from the Samaritan woman that our imperfect stories are the very catalysts God uses to help us recognize our need for Christ. The mic-drop moment in the story happened when Jesus said to the woman, "I AM the Messiah!" (John 4:26). If it were a movie scene, this was when the background music would cease, her eyes would lock onto his, and her heart would explode as a theological conversation became a revelation and a redemption.

In response, the woman immediately "left her water jar beside the well and ran back to the village, telling everyone, 'Come and see a man who told me everything I ever did!'" (John 4:28-29). This is a woman on mission! She wanted to share Jesus with those from her hometown. She is the first recorded Gentile to declare Jesus as the Messiah. The text goes on to say, "Many Samaritans from the village believed in Jesus because the woman had said, 'He told me everything I ever did!'" (John 4:39). They believed that Jesus was "indeed the Savior of the world" (John 4:42) because the Samaritan woman invited them to meet Jesus and listen to his message.

I love this example of being on mission because the woman at the well didn't decide she had to sit through years of teaching on doctrine, or that she had to figure out whether Jews or Samaritans had the best theology about which mountain was the "right choice" for worship. She simply ran to tell everyone she knew about Jesus. The unclean, outcast, unwanted, and unwelcome woman was the very vessel God used to bring living water to parched souls.

No matter what our pasts hold of both pain and regret, no matter how much of the Bible we know, no matter how unlikely it seems that God could meet us right where we are . . . the woman at the well is proof of the promise that God can use each of us to be bold and joyful evangelists of the gospel—because living water doesn't run out.

## The Women at the Resurrection

In our house, there is a lot of joking that goes on among our boys and Josh. They love to play pranks on one another. On one occasion, Josh convinced our middle son, Leland, that he would grow a horn out of his forehead if he didn't eat his vegetables. They rib each other and dream up random stories all the time to try to get a reaction. As the boys have gotten older, they've learned that the quickest way to get to the bottom of whatever yarn their dad is spinning is to ask me whether it's true. If Mom goes along with it, then they know Dad isn't joking.

Mom's words are true.

Unfortunately, trusting the words of a woman wasn't common in the ancient Near East. Women were considered second-class citizens whose sole purpose and identity were found in their husbands and their ability to produce male offspring. Often they weren't protected, cared for, or even considered. This helps us understand how remarkable it was that God chose women, who weren't even able to testify in court as credible witnesses, to be the first witnesses of Jesus' resurrection. Knowing that God entrusted his message to women should cause us to pause, take notice, and pay attention to what God was doing in and through these women.

Here is what the Gospels say about who these women were:

> Mary Magdalene and the other Mary went out to visit the tomb.
> MATTHEW 28:1

Mary Magdalene, Mary the mother of James, and Salome went out and purchased burial spices so they could anoint Jesus' body.

MARK 16:1

The women from Galilee followed and saw the tomb where his body was placed. Then they went home and prepared spices and ointments to anoint his body.

LUKE 23:55-56

These are the same women who faithfully followed, ministered to, and lived alongside Jesus. They journeyed with him on the road to Calvary, even when his disciples had deserted him. They stayed with him through the horrific and excruciating process of his crucifixion (John 19:25). And they were still beside him in the moments when he took his last breath on the cross. Their fear didn't deter them, nor did their deep grief and sadness prevent them from continuing to love Jesus and care for him through their acts of service.

I especially love Mark's account, which offers a glimpse of the actual play-by-play of the women getting everything ready and then trying to figure out as they walked who was going to move the stone from the tomb when they got there (Mark 16:1-3). But these women weren't deterred by logistics; they had done what they could and knew they would figure out the rest. These devoted followers of Jesus were committed to doing the next faithful act to love their teacher and leader well—and in the midst of their small steps of obedience, God changed history in a moment they would never forget or stop talking about.

Matthew includes the conversation that took place between the women and an angel at the tomb:

The angel spoke to the women. "Don't be afraid!" he said. "I know you are looking for Jesus, who was crucified. He isn't here! He is risen from the dead, just as he said would happen. Come, see where his body was lying. And now, go quickly and tell his disciples that he has risen from the dead, and he is going ahead of you to Galilee. You will see him there. Remember what I have told you."

The women ran quickly from the tomb. They were very frightened but also filled with great joy, and they rushed to give the disciples the angel's message.

MATTHEW 28:5-8

In each Gospel account, women were the first at the tomb.

In each Gospel account, it was an angel who told the women that Jesus was not dead but alive.

In each Gospel account, the women were charged to go and share the good news with the disciples.

The women were heralds of a message to the hurting, the despairing, and the doubting. Through the voices of women, joy pierced the dark. They proclaimed the fulfillment of a promise first given in the Garden of Eden—that the coming Messiah would crush the head of the serpent, Satan (Genesis 3:15).

Do you see why it is so significant that God chose women to be the first witnesses to the Resurrection, and the first heralds of hope, victory, and fulfillment? If you and I were writing this story, we probably would have picked the most prominent and influential leaders among Jesus' followers to be the first witnesses. We might have chosen Peter or James or John because they were the closest to Jesus, or perhaps we would have chosen the Roman officials who put Jesus to death in the first place. It seems like a great way to silence the skeptics and prove that God was in charge all along. But instead, God chose the overlooked, the unlikely, the unthought of. He chose to entrust the most valuable message of all to the ones to whom the world ascribed little value.

Centuries later, you and I have the same privilege as the women who first witnessed the Resurrection. God has entrusted us with the good news of hope, joy, and truth. We can boldly proclaim that the tomb is empty, Jesus is alive, death is defeated, and God has fulfilled his promises to us. And sometimes we get to proclaim that good news in the most unlikely of places.

My friend Brenna routinely navigates multiple layers of security at a Texas prison so she can teach Bible studies to women on death row. She sits face-to-face with them and hears their stories of heartbreak, regret, and fear. Then she heralds the message of redemption. Much like the woman at the well who considered herself too far gone until she met Jesus, these women hear the gospel and find hope and healing. The gospel is proclaimed to the prisoners.

My friend Donna is the founder and leader of a reading program in the heart of inner-city Memphis. Through after-school snacks, mentoring, and one-on-one tutoring, children not only gain the skills to be successful in school but also hear the gospel message. As a result, entire families have come to believe in Jesus and be baptized. The gospel is proclaimed in the middle of gang violence, drug abuse, and poverty.

A group of women in our church have a monthly outreach to dancers at a local "gentleman's club." They talk with the women and pray with them. Recently, they were able to host the women for dinner at a local restaurant and learn about their kids and their stories of growing up in incredibly difficult circumstances. Through tear-filled eyes, the dancers expressed their desire to give their kids a better life. As the church women listened and later helped the dancers with everything from looking for better jobs to budgeting, they shared with each woman how valued, loved, and cherished she is by God. As the gospel is proclaimed, the love of God reaches inside the walls of a strip club.

Wherever there are souls on the planet, there is a need to share the gospel message. It might be next door, or it might be across the ocean. Wherever we find ourselves, the words "He is risen!" (Luke 24:6) are the most powerful and life-changing words on the planet. They herald the good news that Jesus has defeated both sin and death and offers us new life.

When it comes to sharing the gospel, the question isn't so much about what you say or how you say it as it is whether you are saying anything at all. What efforts are you making to take the gospel to the ends of the earth? What dark and broken situations are you willing to step into so you are the trusted friend, sister, or neighbor who points someone to their need for Jesus? What hard circumstances are you willing to navigate so you can bring the message of life to those who feel they are living on the edge of death?

I find that when my urgency to share God's message wanes, it's often because I have lost touch with the reality that people are living in spiritual tombs. I have been lulled into the lie of thinking that things aren't so bad and that the pleasures and ease of this life are fulfilling. It usually takes glimpses of the darkness to rebirth within me the urgency to go and tell. When earthquakes devastate entire countries, when conflict and war disperse refugees into stale shelters, when a church member calls to share through a shaky voice that her teenage son was tragically killed in a car accident—these are the sobering moments that become opportunities to share God's life-giving power and grace.

These words of Isaiah are a fitting charge to help us follow our sisters' examples of heralding good news to a broken planet:

How beautiful on the mountains
    are the feet of the messenger who brings good news,
the good news of peace and salvation,
    the news that the God of Israel reigns!
The watchmen shout and sing with joy,
    for before their very eyes
    they see the LORD returning to Jerusalem.

ISAIAH 52:7-8

Or, in the words or Karen Watson, "His glory [our] reward."

## DISCUSSION QUESTIONS

1. What are your associations with missions and missionaries?
   Have you thought of being on mission as something that is
   primarily for others or for everyone?

2. Karen Watson gave her life to share the gospel message of
   Jesus, but even more people heard of her testimony following
   her death. How does her story affect the way you think about
   your own impact when it comes to sharing the gospel?

3. What tends to keep you from sharing the gospel or thinking of
   yourself as being on mission? Is it, for example, busyness, fear,
   or rejection? In what ways did this chapter challenge you to be
   more intentional about being on mission?

4. Karen Watson wrote, "His glory my reward." How does her focus
   on eternity shift your perspective on things like relationships,
   possessions, pursuits, and even your own calling? What attitudes
   and actions need to shift in order to realign your heart with
   God's call on your life?

# 8

# Women and the Church

## Beth Moore

Beekeeper | Bible Teacher | Founder of Living Proof Ministries

Popcorn, Coca-Cola, and the enchantment of a good story on a big screen helped spark Beth Green's love of stories when she was growing up in the small town of Arkadelphia, Arkansas.

At the age of eighteen, Beth felt the Lord calling her into ministry. As a college freshman, she had no idea what that meant or looked like, but she chose to give God her yes.

After graduating from college, Beth married and had two beautiful girls. As a young mom, she juggled preschool pickups and household tasks with teaching a Christian aerobics class. Each week, she led the women in exercise and then taught devotionals. Her yes to God then led to saying yes to teaching a Bible study class at her church, First Baptist in Houston. And that in turn led to another yes to writing homework questions based on her week's lesson.

Little did she know that saying yes to faithfully shepherding and guiding women to study their Bibles was the beginning of a whole new ministry. Living Proof Ministries would ultimately take Beth across the globe to teach, train, and call women to dive deep into the Word of God and live out their God-given callings. She has published more than twenty-five Bible studies in twenty different languages to reach women everywhere.

A few years ago, I was able to attend a conference Beth hosted for twenty- and thirtysomething leaders in Houston, Texas. I listened intently as she charged us to treasure God's Word above all else and to chase him instead of our own platforms and accomplishments. It felt as if she were pulling us in close and pouring out all her motherly wisdom. It reminded me of King David teaching his son Solomon that integrity, character, and intimacy with God would be the only sustaining factors in life and leadership (1 Kings 2:1-4).

Since that conference, I've watched Beth continue to proclaim the truth of God's Word, and I've also watched her endure harsh criticism for her prophetic words against systemic abuse, misogyny, and Christian nationalism. A true Deborah of our day, she has empowered countless women who were hurt and mistreated at the hands of abusers.

When asked how church leadership could do better in empowering women in the local church, she said this:

> I can answer that so simply. Look at Christ with every encounter he has with a woman and emulate that. If in the local church men and women are never serving together, then the respect is never built between the genders. . . . There are ways for men and women to serve with a mutual esteem for one another, and then you

can find out how many gifted women you have in your congregation. I want you to remember what church would have been like if you wiped out all the faithful women Sunday school teachers and women on the mission field. What would we do then?[1]

Beth has modeled, championed, and led the way for countless women to follow in her footsteps as women who are marked by the Word. Her grit, wit, and transparency have paved the way for generations of women to own their place not only in the Kingdom but also within various areas of ministry.

———————— ◉ ————————

O ur family loves to go to the beach in the summertime. For us, summer rest includes everything from the sound of the waves to having sand all over the place to trying to hide our veggie sticks from the hunting seagulls flying overhead. We have many joy-filled memories of our times at the beach.

Over the years, there have been times when, amid their Olympics-worthy boogie boarding or snorkeling escapades, our kids would end up halfway down the shoreline. Then Josh and I had to call and swim after them to bring them back to our little place on the beach. To keep this from continuing, we huddled together and used a sand diagram to come up with what we called our "buoy system." We picked a spot on the shore that spanned the distance of the two buoys out on the water, and the kids were to stay within those boundaries to keep them from ending up too far down the shore. As they swam, every so often they would stop, look for the buoys, and then come back toward the little piece of beach on which we had camped out for the day. Staying within the buoys kept the kids close to us and aware of where they were supposed to be.

Much like a wide-open ocean, the conversation of the role of women in the church can feel like an intimidating and overwhelming topic to tackle. It seems everyone has heated talking points about our calling and value as women. Terms such as *complementarian* and *egalitarian* are thrown around amid a backdrop of stereotypes, personal hurts, and very little desire to understand, all of which ends up stunting much of the conversation and marginalizing women in the name of biblical orthodoxy.

For the longest time, I struggled with how my strong personality and gifts were to be "rightly" used in the church. As a result, I often operated out of fear of doing something wrong rather than walking in the confidence of who God had gifted me to be. As I speak with women about their experiences in the church, they often express how there is a lack of focus on opportunities for women to serve within the church, and that when women *are* addressed in church, the topics are sexual purity before marriage and submission to husbands after marriage. When the news cycle includes repeated stories of abuse, affairs, and power scandals in churches, we know we are in desperate need of looking back to God's original design for the church and for the flourishing of men and women.

Depending on your denomination and faith tradition, you may have felt the sting of being pushed aside and silenced. Now you sit on the proverbial shores watching others exercise their gifts in the ocean of ministry. Or you may feel that you are swimming full steam ahead in serving God and others, and no one can limit your progress or have a say in how you will swim. No doubt there is a huge spectrum of experiences, hurts, and perspectives that comes with this conversation, but my objective isn't to arrive at the one "correct" answer—although I do believe it's vital to study and wrestle with your understanding of Scripture. Instead, my hope is to focus on what constitutes the "buoys" for healthy ministry by exploring, re-centering, and celebrating the work of God through women in the church. And in one chapter of his letter to the Romans, the apostle Paul mentioned many women in the early church who provided compelling role models for us to follow.

## Romans 16

In his letter to the Romans, the apostle Paul mentioned nearly thirty people whom he considered co-laborers, fellow servants, and ministry leaders. Of those, ten were women.

Pause for a second and let that sink in. One of the greatest missionaries and preachers of all time invites an entire church to join him in acknowledging, thanking, edifying, and celebrating the work of both men and women who have worked alongside him in ministry.

When we are looking at the buoys of what healthy churches and church cultures look like, this is pivotal. From the beginning of Creation, men and women are given equal worth, dignity, and value. However, when we think of equality today, we tend to think more in terms of things being exactly the same for men and women, or in terms of fairness and opportunity. However, a larger picture of equality provides a picture of "being with" and togetherness that was present in both Adam and Eve as they reflected the relational harmony of God the Father, Son, and Holy Spirit. Paul's list of co-laborers in Romans 16 portrays a colorful and multidimensional canvas of such "being with" in ministry. He mentions men and women from different ethnicities, cultural backgrounds, and social classes who minister alongside one another for the cause of Christ.

Our first buoy or marker is to ask the question, "Are men and women both in the waters of ministry?" As you look at the leadership structure of your church or denomination, how many women are there? How often do you hear the stories and voices of women in Sunday sermons? In board meetings and throughout high-level decision-making, how are women's perspectives and strengths being leveraged for the strength of the organization and health of the church overall?

For women to be seen, empowered, and celebrated in the church, we have to be intentional in creating structures, systems, and ministry opportunities that include them. Whenever there is an absence of men or women, we are not fully displaying the image of God in our orthodoxy (what we believe) or our orthopraxy (how we live out what we believe).

Our next buoy question should then be, "How did women serve in the early church?" To answer that question, I want to focus on Romans 16, the chapter in which Paul mentioned ten women who served alongside him in the early church.

Paul first mentioned Phoebe:

> I commend to you our sister Phoebe, who is a deacon in the church in Cenchrea. Welcome her in the Lord as one who is worthy of honor among God's people. Help her in whatever she needs, for she has been helpful to many, and especially to me.
>
> ROMANS 16:1-2

Paul, the leader of the Gentile church, entrusted Phoebe, a woman, to carry and read his letter to the church at Rome.[2] This is huge! Paul's letter to the Romans is arguably the richest, longest, and theologically deepest letter he wrote. This wasn't a quick-hello, fix-this, don't-do-that, and I'll-see-you-soon type of letter. It was a substantive letter that has become one of the most studied and debated books throughout church history. And it was first held, carried, and read aloud by a woman.

Phoebe was also described as a sister and a deacon. The familial descriptor meant she was not less than or second class but part of the family. The Greek word translated as "deacon" is *diakonos*, the same word used elsewhere in Scripture for male deacons in the church. Theologians differ on Phoebe's specific role, but it is likely she had a recognized position and ministry within the church. Notice also how Paul said that she had "been *helpful* to many, and especially to me" (Romans 16:2, italics added). Phoebe's presence and position in the early church demonstrate that Paul esteemed her ministry just as much as he did the ministry of the men who served in the church.

Paul goes on to mention Priscilla, whom we have already read about: "Give my greetings to Priscilla and Aquila, my co-workers in the ministry of Christ Jesus" (Romans 16:3). It was Priscilla and Aquila who taught Apollos the Scriptures (Acts 18:24-26). It is interesting to note that Paul mentioned Priscilla before her husband, which would have been notable in the Roman world. Is this an indication that she is better or more important than her husband? Not at all. Paul's intentional wording would simply have drawn his readers' attention to both of their contributions and elevated Priscilla to a position of honor and esteem within the church. Paul went on to say, "They once risked their lives for me. I am thankful to them, and so are all the Gentile churches" (Romans 16:4). Priscilla and Aquila were pillars of the faith to many men and women who followed them.

The next woman whom Paul acknowledged was Mary: "Give my greetings to Mary, who has worked so hard for your benefit" (Romans 16:6). Paul affirmed Mary for her diligence and for pouring herself out for the benefit of the Roman church.

Next in Paul's list of women was Junia. The risks she took to follow Jesus landed her in a Roman prison: "Greet Andronicus and Junia, my fellow Jews, who were in prison with me. They are highly respected among the apostles and became followers of Christ before I did" (Romans 16:7). The fact that both Andronicus and Junia were highly esteemed by the apostles indicates that she was known and recognized for her work and for her devotion to God and the apostles' teaching.

Paul also acknowledged Tryphena, Tryphosa, and Persis: "Give my greetings to Tryphena and Tryphosa, the Lord's workers, and to dear Persis, who has worked so hard for the Lord" (Romans 16:12). Paul's characterization of the women as fellow workers in the Lord echoes the theme of "being with" from Genesis 2 as they labored together.

Although he doesn't give her name, Paul mentioned Rufus's mother: "Greet Rufus, whom the Lord picked out to be his very own; and also his dear mother, who has been a mother to me" (Romans 16:13). In none of his writings did Paul provide any information about his own mother, and yet here he specifically mentioned the mother of Rufus as being a mother to him. We don't know much about Rufus, but we do have one clue. In Mark's account of the Crucifixion, he mentioned how Jesus was aided on his walk to Calvary: "A passerby named Simon, who was from Cyrene, was coming in from the countryside just then, and the soldiers forced him to carry Jesus' cross. (Simon was the father of Alexander and Rufus.)" (Mark 15:21). It is such a beautiful connection! In his final journey, to the cross, Jesus was ministered to by Rufus's father, Simon. Years later, Rufus and his mother would minister to and serve alongside a radically transformed persecutor of the church named Paul, and they would treat him as if he were part of their own family. God's act of weaving the threads of Rufus's family's lives together with Paul's life is so purposeful that you can't help but think of how grand and big God's plan is.

Paul concluded his list of greetings, mentioning two more women: Julia and Nereus's sister. He then exhorted all the believers to "greet each other with a sacred kiss" (Romans 16:16). For the church, this greeting was a physical representation of the love, care, and common bond that united the family of faith.

We often think of the church as characterized by a building, a set of traditions, and a list of songs sung on a Sunday morning. But the reality is that those who have been redeemed and adopted into the family of God are the church. We are a people, not a place, and the people who make up the local church are families of men and women, young and old, with different stories and struggles, but all with the same goal and desire to make Jesus known.

## The Church as the Bride

Just as Jesus was revolutionary in the way that he invited, elevated, and ministered to and alongside women, he also used the compelling image of a bride to characterize his deep love for the church.

The apostle Paul picked up on this imagery in his letter to the church at Ephesus when he instructed husbands and wives how to love one another:

> Submit to one another out of reverence for Christ.
>
> For wives, this means submit to your husbands as to the Lord. For a husband is the head of his wife as Christ is the head of the church. He is the Savior of his body, the church. As the church submits to Christ, so you wives should submit to your husbands in everything.
>
> For husbands, this means love your wives, just as Christ loved the church. He gave up his life for her to make her holy and clean, washed by the cleansing of God's word. He did this to present her to himself as a glorious church without a spot or wrinkle or any other blemish. Instead, she will be holy and without fault. In the same

way, husbands ought to love their wives as they love their own bodies. For a man who loves his wife actually shows love for himself. No one hates his own body but feeds and cares for it, just as Christ cares for the church.

EPHESIANS 5:21-29

Although the text speaks to both husbands and wives, more attention is often paid to the statement that wives are to submit to husbands (which follows Paul's first statement that we are all to submit to one another, but that is a discussion for another day). Paul draws a parallel between wives and the bride of Christ to focus in on the love and honor Christ shows to his bride, the church. He sacrifices himself and cleanses, purifies, redeems, pursues, protects, cares for, and ultimately dies for her to be in right standing with God.

As the bride of Christ, we are washed clean, pursued, and protected by our Bridegroom, and in that relationship and freedom, we are to live without fear of rejection, abandonment, or mistreatment. Instead, we can totally abandon ourselves to the love that transformed our lives.

The final book of the Bible includes these words: "The Spirit and the bride say, 'Come.' Let anyone who hears this say, 'Come.' Let anyone who is thirsty come. Let anyone who desires drink freely from the water of life" (Revelation 22:17). Doesn't this remind you of our friend, the Samaritan woman at the well?

As members of the body of Christ, we labor, minister, love, and share the good news of our Groom, who has sanctified us and is coming again for our wedding feast.

## Changing the Conversation

One of the flaws in how we approach the Bible is that we come to it with our own preconceived ideas and questions rather than allowing the text to form the questions we bring to it. For example, we might come to Scripture asking, "What are women allowed to do?" And yet I don't see that question being asked in Scripture. What I see throughout the metanarrative of Scripture, and I hope what you have seen thus far in this book, is that there are clear ways in which both men and women reflect the attributes of God, both as individuals and in partnership with each other in ministry. We are called to mutual mission, and to minister alongside one another in both our strengths and our weaknesses. In the process, we not only remind one another of our need for the kind of togetherness that was evident back in Eden, but also of our fundamental need to embody harmony, love, and respect in a continually fractured and broken world. That is our role as sons and daughters of God.

So, going back to the buoy analogy, what are some of the markers we can look to when we consider women in the church?

- We know that both men and women are to work and reflect the image of God.
- We know that God has made us to work and serve alongside one another as part of the Great Commission.
- We know that men and women bring unique distinctions that reflect God's image.
- We know that men and women walk out their gifts in a familial relationship and do so for the good of one another.
- We know that the absence of either men or women in the organizational structure of the church means that we are not wholly reflecting who God wants us to be.
- We know that equality does not mean exact or interchangeable involvement.

Just as there is a distinction in the forming of man and woman in Genesis 2, that distinction plays out within the church by setting aside the office of elder/bishop/pastor for qualified male leadership. Paul speaks to this distinction and the qualifications of male pastors and elders in both 2 Timothy and Titus. These qualified brothers are called to shepherd, protect, guide, and equip the church for the work of Christ as they reflect the character and honor of Christ to those God has entrusted to them. This means that outside of this office, women are able to lead, teach, serve, and love in the same way the faithful sisters in Romans 16 lived out their giftedness in the early church.

So if these are our buoys and the buoys are for our good, then just as Genesis says, our question shifts from "Why can't I do that?" to "How do I serve freely within the buoys?" There is so much freedom when we trust that God's good design for us, for our brothers, and for the church is what helps to bring about our own flourishing.

There is a whole ocean of ministry to experience: The distinct taste of the salt water as you come up for air. The resistance of the water as you stroke through it and the opportunity to explore the colors and wildlife below. The sound of the waves crashing the gritty sand between your toes.

There is beauty everywhere you go. Look for the buoys; then dive in!

## DISCUSSION QUESTIONS

1. What positive or negative experiences have you had in the local church while ministering alongside your brothers in Christ? How have those experiences impacted your willingness and desire to serve in the local church?

2. As we look at women in the Bible and explore our own callings, why is it important that we continue to make an effort to work alongside our brothers in Christ?

3. How does Paul's mention of so many women in his letter to the Roman church encourage you about the need for women to actively use their gifts in ministry?

4. Who are the women you have watched serve in ministry ahead of you? What have you learned from them?

5. What insecurities or fears keep you from fully serving with your gifts? In what ways would you like to serve as part of following God's call for your life?

# 9

# Women and Justice
# for the Vulnerable

## Rachael Denhollander

Gymnast | Advocate | Attorney

Rachael Denhollander grew up in Kalamazoo, Michigan, and
was one of many girls who loved the flips, turns, twists, and
athleticism of being a gymnast. Tragically, the sport she loved
became a source of deep loss and trauma. But it also became
her platform to be an advocate and a voice for the voiceless.

As a teen gymnast, Rachael was one of hundreds of women
and girls abused at the hands of Dr. Larry Nassar, who was the
team doctor for the women's US gymnastics national team.
Like many abuse victims, it would be years before Rachael and
others would come forward to report their abuse. In college, she
decided to become a lawyer. Later, with her giftings and through
God's divine plan, she became the leader, voice, and advocate for
countless women who had experienced sexual abuse.

Rachael first shared her abuse with the Michigan police and then with the *Indianapolis Star*. She was the first to speak out publicly against not only Nassar but also the systemic problems within the gymnastics culture. Her courage and advocacy gave dignity and strength to more than 250 others who would follow in her steps. Olympians such as Simone Biles, Gabby Douglas, and Aly Raisman boldly stood before Nassar in a crowded courtroom and testified against him.

In her victim impact statement, Rachael stood at a podium with a watching world listening as she spoke poignantly of the evil of abuse. And along with the bitter sting and somber truth of the words she spoke, she also extended grace as she pointed to the mercy of Jesus. She directed her remarks to both Larry Nassar and to the judge, Rosemarie Aquilina, sharing the depth of her trauma and her hopes for healing:

> I want you to understand why I made this choice knowing full well what it was going to cost to get here and with very little hope of ever succeeding. I did it because it was right. No matter the cost, it was right. And the farthest I can run from what you [Nassar] have become is to daily choose what is right instead of what I want. . . .
>
> The Bible you speak [of] carries a final judgment where all of God's wrath and eternal terror is poured out on men like you. Should you ever reach the point of truly facing what you have done, the guilt will be crushing. And that is what makes the gospel of Christ so sweet. Because it extends grace and hope and mercy where none should be found. And it will be there for you.
>
> I pray you experience the soul crushing weight of guilt so you may someday experience true repentance and true forgiveness from God, which you need far more

than forgiveness from me—though I extend that to you as well. . . .

I ask that you [Judge Aquilina] hand down a sentence that tells us that what was done to us matters, that we are known, we are worth everything, worth the greatest protection the law can offer, the greatest measure of justice available.

And to everyone who is watching, I ask that same question, how much is a little girl worth?[1]

Rachael continues to advocate for abuse survivors and is the author of a memoir, *What Is a Girl Worth?* and a children's book, *How Much Is a Little Girl Worth?* She lives in Michigan with her husband, Jacob, and their four children.

———————— ◉ ————————

Accoording to my therapist, I have "justice issues." As a kid, I was the little girl on the playground who lectured the group of kids who were bullying another group of kids. As an adult, my justice issues occasionally take the form of Twitter debates that tend to end up with me throwing my hands up in frustration and wondering why everyone else can't just see it the way I see it.

Mother Teresa has been credited with the saying, "Justice without love is not justice. Love without justice is not love." In a culture too often polarized about both the causes and cures for injustice, it's easy to forget that God's character holds together both justice and love. They aren't contradictory but are both extensions of a holy and righteous God.

If we as women who are redeemed and made new in Jesus are to reflect the character of God in our communities, workplaces, homes, and neighborhoods, then part of that reflection requires that we seek out, minister to, love, and fight for the vulnerable, outcast, poor, and marginalized. We must take our place with women from biblical history who risked their lives to stand for God and for good in the face of injustice. To start, we can learn from the examples of Shiphrah and Puah, Jael, and Dorcas.

## Shiphrah and Puah

To understand the significance of Shiphrah and Puah, we first need to understand the background events leading up to their story.

At the end of the book of Genesis, Joseph, who was still living in Egypt and second in power only to Pharaoh, reminded his brothers that even though he was about to die, God would fulfill his promises and take them to the land he had promised to Abraham and his descendants. After Joseph took his last breath, he was embalmed and entombed in Egypt.

The story picks up in the first chapter of Exodus, beginning with a list of the sons of Jacob (Joseph's father), noting that his descendants were fruitful and increased rapidly. Then comes this ominous statement: "Eventually, a new king came to power in Egypt who knew nothing about Joseph or what he had done" (Exodus 1:8).

The new pharaoh demanded that the Israelites be treated harshly. Out of fear that they would rise up and overthrow Egypt, he oppressed them.

- They were made slaves and ruled over by brutal slave masters (Exodus 1:11).
- They were subjected to crushing labor without mercy (Exodus 1:13).
- The Egyptians made their lives bitter and were ruthless in their demands (Exodus 1:14).

The Israelites' days were full of agony, oppression, deep darkness, and pain. It is easy for us to read right past this narrative of hardship because we know that God ultimately delivered them and that Pharaoh and his men were drowned in the sea, but we need to sit in the reality that they lived under the heavy burden of hopelessness, had questions and misgivings about when God would rescue them, and no doubt wondered whether they even believed in God's promises anymore. They knew that God had saved Jacob and his family through Joseph. They knew that Joseph had served right alongside Pharaoh for decades, and that God had provided life and protection not only for the Israelites but also for the whole region. So where was God now? Who was going to save them?

Just when it seemed as if the hard, heavy, and ruthless mistreatment couldn't get any worse, a new decree went out to the Hebrew midwives: "When you help the Hebrew women as they give birth, watch as they deliver. If the baby is a boy, kill him" (Exodus 1:16). The innocent coos and cries of newborn baby boys would now be met with blood and tears.

This is where two of the Hebrew midwives, Shiphrah and Puah, entered the story. Here is how the text describes their response to the king's decree: "Because the midwives feared God, they refused to obey the king's orders. They allowed the boys to live, too" (Exodus 1:17). These two women—who were likely the leaders of what some scholars estimate may have been up to five hundred Hebrew midwives—are known for their fear of God. They feared God more than they feared for their own lives. They were solely concerned with following Yahweh and protecting life, even if it meant losing their own.

Can you imagine what went through their minds when they were subsequently summoned to account for their actions?

Exodus 1:18 says, "The king of Egypt called for the midwives. 'Why have you done this?' he demanded. 'Why have you allowed the boys to live?'" The two women, together, stood before the most powerful ruler on the planet knowing full well that they had disobeyed a direct command. As I imagine it, I can feel the heaviness of each step of the palace guards as they surrounded Shiphrah and Puah, bringing them closer and closer to their death sentence. I wonder if they whispered the names of the baby boys they had saved, reassuring each other that it had been worth it. I wonder if they prayed to be spared or to die faithfully.

As it happened, God spared their lives and blessed their obedience by giving them families of their own (Exodus 1:21). God also blessed the Israelites, who "continued to multiply, growing more and more powerful" (Exodus 1:20). Shiphrah and Puah's obedience multiplied into the salvation of an untold number of lives. In their own way, these two brave midwives fulfilled God's command to be fruitful and multiply by protecting life, advocating for life, and standing up for life.

## Jael

Jael is another tucked-away character who is often overlooked but whose bravery impacted generations. She was a tentmaker and the wife of Heber the Kenite. The name Jael means mountain goat, which probably doesn't make you want to name your next daughter after her, but maybe after digging into her story, you might change your mind.

Jael's story took place when Israel was once more stuck in a cycle of sin and idolatry. Consequently, God allowed the nation to be turned over to King Jabin, a Canaanite, who "ruthlessly oppressed the Israelites for twenty years" (Judges 4:3). Sound familiar? This time, God used a prophetess named Deborah, whose story we'll explore in the next chapter, to free Israel from the oppression of yet another ruthless dictator.

King Jabin had an army commander named Sisera. While Israel attacked and killed Sisera's army, Sisera fled on foot to escape the war. Enter Jael. Because there was peace between Jael's people and Sisera, he sought refuge and safety in her tent. Weary from the battle, he entered her tent and was given milk, rest, and even a blanket to comfort him in his retreat. What happens next is something for the movies.

> When Sisera fell asleep from exhaustion, Jael quietly crept up to him with a hammer and tent peg in her hand. Then she drove the tent peg through his temple and into the ground, and so he died.
>
> JUDGES 4:21

This tender and seemingly compassionate woman who was supposed to be giving rest, protection, and respite to an army general was now the slayer of Sisera. The turn of events causes readers to question what caused Jael to turn on Sisera and what would prompt such a violent reaction toward him, especially if there was peace between their peoples.

Deborah said in her recounting of the story that Jael was the most blessed among tent-dwelling women. Here is her song:

> From the window Sisera's mother looked out.
>     Through the window she watched for his return, saying,
>     "Why is his chariot so long in coming?
>     Why don't we hear the sound of chariot wheels?"
>     Her wise women answer,
>         and she repeats these words to herself:

"They must be dividing the captured plunder—
   with a woman or two for every man.
There will be colorful robes for Sisera,
   and colorful, embroidered robes for me.
Yes, the plunder will include
   colorful robes embroidered on both sides."
LORD, may all your enemies die like Sisera!
   But may those who love you rise like the sun in all its
      power!

JUDGES 5:28-31

Did you catch that? Sisera's idea of dividing the plunder was to divvy up the women between himself and his soldiers, to be raped and used. In that day, women were considered spoils of war, little more than a means for physical pleasure.

At the end of her song, the text notes, "Then there was peace in the land for forty years" (Judges 5:31). Because of the courage and bravery of Jael and Deborah, the people of Israel not only escaped yet another evil oppressor but also lived in peace for forty years. The Hebrew word translated "peace" in this verse is not *shalom* but *shaqat*, which means to be quiet, to rest, or to be undisturbed. Israel's frequent turmoil, fear, and oppression was exchanged for rest, stillness, and peace.

## Dorcas

We have seen that God secured justice by using courageous women to protect life and fight oppressors. Now we turn our attention to a woman who secured justice by caring for the marginalized. Her name is Dorcas.

Dorcas made something of a dramatic entrance in Scripture when Peter raised her from the dead, but if we look at the few verses that tell her story, I think we will discover why this servant leader was so beloved in her community.

The text says, "She was always doing kind things for others and helping the poor" (Acts 9:36). Her heartbeat for the poor, vulnerable, and downcast reflected the heart of her Savior. The literal translation of the Greek is that she was "full of good works and doing acts of mercy." The tense of the Greek verbs also suggests that she did these things continually rather than simply at occasional moments.

Dorcas was the ancient version of that woman in your church who is always hopping around town getting groceries for the shut-ins, making calls to get donations for the local food pantry, and spending her weekend making meals for her grandkids and all the neighborhood friends they play with. She was always showing up to give of her time, energy, and resources for the benefit of others.

We see her legacy in the grief and testimonies of a roomful of widows who, after Dorcas had become ill and died, showed Peter all the coats and clothes that she had stitched with love (Acts 9:39). It is worth noting that no family members were mentioned as being present at the scene of her passing and the subsequent mourning, but as we have already discussed, the church is family, and those who felt the grief of losing Dorcas were those to whom she had ministered.

When Peter prayed and commanded Dorcas to get up from her deathbed, the text says, "She opened her eyes! When she saw Peter, she sat up! He gave her his hand and helped her up. Then he called in the widows and all the believers, and he presented her to them alive" (Acts 9:40-41).

Dorcas never expected to receive anything in return for her ministry to the poor. There was no way for the poor to repay her. And yet God's love was made manifest in her because of the poor. Mother Teresa once said, "Only in heaven will we see how much we owe to the poor for helping us to love God better because of them."[2]

Dorcas, who created beautiful coverings for the forgotten and expected nothing in return, was a picture of what God has done for us through Jesus Christ. The widows, along with many others throughout the town of Joppa, believed in the Lord because of the life and ministry of Dorcas.

There is an interesting parallel between the clothing or coverings mentioned in the story of Dorcas and the coverings in the story of Adam and Eve in the Garden of Eden. When sin broke their fellowship with God, death entered the world, Adam and Eve's relationship was fractured, and they felt the need to hide and cover themselves because of shame. With Dorcas, it is the testimony of the widows about the coverings she made for them that clothed them in dignity, brought them into community, and became part of her story of being raised from the dead.

When you and I think of the legacy we want to leave behind, we tend to think of security for our families or being someone with a good name.

But what if, like Dorcas, we focused only on seeing and ministering to those the world has chosen not to see?

What if, like Dorcas, we used our gifts and abilities to create provision for and show honor to those less fortunate than us?

What if, like Dorcas, we pointed women to Jesus and the life he gives rather than to our own aspirations and accomplishments?

## Mrs. Janice

Mrs. Janice was a lady in one of the churches where my husband and I once served. She was the widow of a well-known evangelist and pastor named Walter. Mrs. Janice spent most of her adult life traveling with her husband and seeing God save and transform countless people who surrendered to the gospel.

I loved listening to her quirky and sometimes hard-to-follow stories of how she and Walter traveled the United States together attending tent revivals and church gatherings of all sizes. My favorite was the story of her wedding. With a wide grin and laughter, she shared that after fifty-plus years of marriage, it turned out that she and Walter weren't *actually* married. One afternoon, without their parents knowing, Janice, Walter, and a preacher friend stood on a bridge that connected Texas to Arkansas. The couple exchanged vows and said "I do"; just like that, they were married. No big wedding, fancy dress, or even a marriage certificate—just the innocence of young love and their full lives ahead of them.

When I met Janice, she had been a widow for more than a decade, and her love for the church and for others hadn't diminished in her season of singleness. In fact, it kindled brighter and with more fervor. She taught a Sunday school class for older adults that she often jokingly referred to as "The Last Stop," because it was the last class anyone in it would attend before they met Jesus face-to-face. In her words, "I wanted to make sure as many were going with me as I could."

She had this beautiful ability to quilt, and she made countless quilts year after year for all kinds of people. She stitched them for mothers who had lost their sons and daughters in war. She placed patterns and colors together for women with cancer who would wrap themselves up as they endured nauseating chemo treatments.

I had asked her to teach me how to quilt so I could pass the time as we worked toward bringing home our third son, Amos, from Ethiopia. I brought my fabric and my sewing machine and met her in a back room of our church. There, she taught me all about batting, stabilizer, thread count, and how to make my own binding. I kept waiting for her to show me how to sew the strips of colors together, and much to my surprise, she said, "Honey, we are hand quilting this blanket. You can put that machine away."

I thought, *This project is going to take me a lot longer than I anticipated.* And it did. But it was also an act of love that took the form of crooked stitches and hand-tied knots that connected layers of fabric, stabilizer, and batting. To this day, when I look at the quilt in my Amos's room, I think of Mrs. Janice and what I learned from her life and our time together. The lessons weren't so much in the finished blanket but instead in the hands that lovingly pieced it together. The lessons weren't in how to place patterns but in the stories she shared. The lessons weren't in the stitches but in the time she gave to teach, see, and share with a young pastor's wife. These are invaluable and priceless gifts to give.

There are women across the planet who spend their time seeking out and fighting for the vulnerable. For example, organizations such as Women of Welcome gather women to care for and meet needs for refugees and immigrants.

A21 is a ministry that fights to end human trafficking, with efforts in the United States, Europe, South Africa, Southeast Asia, and Australia. Of an estimated 40.3 million people currently enslaved in forced labor or sex trafficking, 71 percent are women and 25 percent are children.[3]

Organizations such as the Psalm 139 Project help to raise money to provide state-of-the-art imaging and ultrasound machines so that women facing an unplanned pregnancy can see the heartbeat, face, and form of their child.

All these organizations are led by women who are modern-day Shiphrahs, Puahs, Jaels, and Dorcases. They have seen, heard, and witnessed the abuse, mistreatment, and deception the enemy has used to steal and wreck lives, and each leader leverages her energy, intellect, influence, time, and resources to wage war on the darkness.

These are women of courage, conviction, and grit.

May we be women who fear God more than we fear man.

May we be women who speak out for the worth and dignity of all people as image bearers.

May we be women who see and serve those whom the world chooses to ignore.

May we be women who stand in the gap for those who have had innocence and dignity stolen from them.

May we be women who welcome the fatherless and give them homes.

May we be women who look the serpent in the eye and bravely declare ourselves agents of gospel redemption.

## DISCUSSION QUESTIONS

1. Is there anything in your story that God has used to birth a desire to help fight for justice as Rachael Denhollander has? What advocacy or care ministries draw your attention? What local organizations can you partner with?

2. Throughout salvation history, God has used women to fight against sin and the impact of sin. How have you seen women pushing back darkness in practical ways?

3. As we look at the story of the midwives Shiphrah and Puah and the story of Jael, we see risk coupled with courage and a willingness to stand for truth. What contemporary issues need women who are willing to take risks and stand for truth?

4. How is the meaning of **ezer**, which we studied in chapter 2, embodied in the protection and strength shown by the women in this chapter who fight for justice and for the vulnerable?

# 10

# Women and Leadership

**Jenny Yang**

Refugee Advocate | World Relief SVP of Advocacy and Policy | Policy Writer

Jenny Yang grew up in Philadelphia, the daughter of immigrants. Her father, orphaned not long after the Korean War, had come to the United States to pursue his dream of fixing cars. Jenny was always aware of the challenges of growing up as what she called a "hyphenated American," or a Korean American, but those challenges also birthed within her a love and appreciation for both cultures and the diversity and beauty she saw in the people around her.

In college, her love of culture, history, and politics led her to study abroad in Spain and to volunteer there for SOS Racismo, an antiracism organization. It was through this experience that she learned an important lesson: Addressing issues of injustice required making changes at both the community level and the systemic level. Later she landed a job with World Relief, a global Christian humanitarian organization. She started out as a case manager in their refugee resettlement program, but after witnessing the challenges refugees faced, she wanted to focus on public policy issues.

Jenny's work in public policy has put her in meeting rooms with US elected officials, as well as some of the world's most powerful and influential leaders. She shares with them her wisdom and her love for refugees, immigrants, and the most vulnerable. Speaking of her work, Jenny says,

> I like convincing people in positions of power to take bold positions that help those who are vulnerable. I love the idea that once you get a bill passed or a policy changed, it impacts thousands of lives. I also like engaging churches to use their voice in the public square because our values belong there. Whenever Christians don't speak up or use their voice, there is a vacuum created in which those who do not represent our values shape the policies that impact all of us. We have a responsibility to advocate for laws that reflect our values, and we also have a responsibility to steward the influence that God has given us to shape a society that reflects dignity for all.[1]

Jenny is an enthusiastic advocate for women to be involved in shaping public policy. She encourages women to own their personal stories and experiences, and then to use them to shape their calling and vocation in life.

> Being a voice for those who are vulnerable doesn't mean you need to run for office (although some should). It could mean speaking up when you feel like a local

school isn't making a right decision, sharing information about a passion of yours, or simply talking to your kids about everyday matters and events that may be easy to overlook. Be bold in who God made you to be. Then reach out and find a community of conspirators and collaborators to do the work together! I've found the most meaningful community with people who have similar passions and joys. We share our platforms, help inform each other's audiences, check in with each other and pray for one another.[2]

Jenny now serves as senior vice president of advocacy and policy at World Relief. In this role, she oversees advocacy initiatives and policy positions and leads their public relations efforts. She is also coauthor of *Welcoming the Stranger: Justice, Compassion, and Truth in the Immigration Debate*.

———————— ◉ ————————

Who doesn't like a solid backup plan? I'm a self-proclaimed type A personality and have great appreciation for a well-thought-out plan behind a plan. In fact, I sometimes have not just one but three or four backup plans. When I was pregnant with our firstborn, Haddon, and our due date was closely approaching, I was more than overprepared. I had a hospital bag at home, a hospital bag in the car, and a hospital bag at work. There wasn't a place I could go where I wasn't prepared. Well, except for that one Sunday evening when we decided to take Josh's truck rather than my car to the Christmas cantata, and my water broke as we were exiting the sanctuary! I didn't think about packing a hospital bag for his car too.

Given the nature and purpose of a backup plan—which is to provide, well, a backup—it isn't necessarily used very much. We can determine how good a backup plan is only when the original plan fails (or the first three fail). Sadly, there are some in the church who have a backup plan mentality when it comes to women and leadership.

As a young woman in church, I often heard the message that I needed to tone down my personality, and that while I could use my strengths and leadership abilities in the "secular world," I needed to set those gifts aside and submit when it came to the church and the home. I have a vivid memory of a conversation with my youth pastor about women and leadership. He proudly told me how he had walked out of a conference where Beth Moore was speaking because he didn't believe in women teaching men. Later, when I asked him about Deborah leading in Israel and how God had used her, he said, "Deborah was allowed to be a judge only because there weren't any godly men who were stepping up. Because the men weren't leading, God used a woman." In other words, Deborah was the backup plan. The message was clear: If I wanted to be a leader, the best I could hope for was to be ready and able to step in and lead if there weren't any men available for the job. And sometimes, on my worst days, I was hoping for the men to fail.

I recently heard of a comment made by a pastor after the appointment of Amy Coney Barrett to the US Supreme Court: "It would still be better if the position were filled by a man." He said this despite the fact that Barrett is highly qualified, has a résumé full of achievements, and holds convictions he shares about protecting life and religious liberty.

Such low views of women result in not only a misrepresentation of men and women working together for the betterment of a church and community, but also the inadvertent bolstering of the sins of sexism, personal abuse, and abuse of power. When ideologies that women are less than are believed and perpetuated, gifted, strong, and talented women are marginalized, looked down on, and even considered a threat. Abuse and mistreatment are all products of this type of thinking, and the result is that individual women are sidelined and organizational systems and leadership structures weakened.

Standing in contrast to all of this are the stories of strong and capable women in Scripture. I am so thankful God intentionally included them in the Bible—in their brokenness and strengths, in their service and their leadership—so we could see them using their God-given spiritual gifts. In studying their stories, I've learned that I don't need to be the backup plan, waiting on the sidelines for my turn. I can be an active participant in the church, in God's mission of bringing about his Kingdom. Three of my favorite examples of women in the Bible who did this are Deborah, Huldah, and Esther.

## Deborah

We first meet Deborah in chapter 4 of the book of Judges. Joshua, the leader who brought the people into the Promised Land, had died, and the Israelites had fallen back into idolatry by worshiping Baal. In judgment, God had turned them over to their enemies. It was a vicious cycle of sin, judgment, repentance, and redemption. And yet God continued to rescue and restore them.

> Whenever the LORD raised up a judge over Israel,
> he was with that judge and rescued the people from
> their enemies throughout the judge's lifetime. For the
> LORD took pity on his people, who were burdened by
> oppression and suffering.
> JUDGES 2:18

God graciously gave his people Othniel, Ehud, and Shamgar as judges. When Israel disobeyed God and worshiped idols, each judge called the people to repentance. God then delivered them from their enemies, but their contrition never lasted long, and Israel would once again commit evil in the Lord's sight. However, the next judge in the queue after Ehud's death is something of a surprise—a woman rather than a man.

> Deborah, the wife of Lappidoth, was a prophet who
> was judging Israel at that time. She would sit under the
> Palm of Deborah, between Ramah and Bethel in the hill
> country of Ephraim, and the Israelites would go to her for
> judgment.
>
> JUDGES 4:4-5

There is no line in Scripture that says, "There were no godly men in Israel, so God settled for Deborah." The text simply describes Israel's continuing sin issues (Judges 4:1) and how God used another judge to show his grace and deliverance. Deborah is described as being a wife, a prophet, and a judge—not a backup plan.

Here is a passage from Bible scholar Herbert Lockyer's description of her:

> Deborah is one of several females in Scripture
> distinguished as being endowed with the prophetic
> gift, which means the ability to discern the mind and
> purpose of God and declare it to others. In the days of
> the Old Testament, prophets and prophetesses were the
> media between God and His people Israel, and their gift
> to perceive and proclaim divine truth stamped them as

being divinely inspired. Such an office, whether held by a male or female, was a high one and corresponds to the ministry of the Word today.[3]

As a prophetess and judge, Deborah spoke the words of God, and people came to her for wisdom, advice, and hope amid darkness and despair. The oppressive reign of King Jabin and his commander, Sisera, had left many deep in their sin and disobedience, and Deborah was strong and resolute in leading her people back to God's mercy and securing their freedom.

She summoned Israel's military leader, Barak, and said,

This is what the LORD, the God of Israel, commands you: Call out 10,000 warriors from the tribes of Naphtali and Zebulun at Mount Tabor. And I will call out Sisera, commander of Jabin's army, along with his chariots and warriors, to the Kishon River. There I will give you victory over him.

JUDGES 4:6-7

Barak's respect for Deborah is evident in his response: "I will go, but only if you go with me" (Judges 4:8). Notice how the verses that follow emphasize Deborah's "going with":

"Very well," she replied, "I will *go with* you. But you will receive no honor in this venture, for the LORD's victory over Sisera will be at the hands of a woman." So Deborah *went with* Barak to Kedesh. At Kedesh, Barak called together the tribes of Zebulun and Naphtali, and 10,000 warriors went up with him. Deborah also *went with* him.

JUDGES 4:9-10, ITALICS ADDED

The text conveys the strength and help of a woman used by God not only to come alongside Barak with encouragement, but also to plan and execute a military conquest. Her role in freeing God's people provides a beautiful echo of the Garden—she is an *ezer* woman, called to be a strong leader and helper.

Deborah could have easily charged Barak to be the leader he was supposed to be and told him to go into battle on his own, but instead she bolstered his courage, rallied the troops to go with him, and ultimately secured God's deliverance of his people. She could also have seen Barak's weakness and wavering as an opportunity to step in and be the hero, and yet she led within the role and attributes God had given her.

Deborah is the embodiment of the *ezer* woman who comes alongside in strength, discernment, and courage. She didn't subvert or diminish Barak's role or responsibility, but with her presence and confidence, they together led the nation to freedom. Her leadership was the catalyst that invigorated Barak and the nation of Israel to fight oppression and step into liberty.

## Huldah

Prior to being led by judges, Israel had been led by kings. After the reign of David's son Solomon, the nation split into two kingdoms—the northern kingdom of Israel and southern kingdom of Judah. Both were known for falling into idolatry by worshiping the pagan gods of neighboring nations. Israel was attacked by the Assyrians as judgment for their disobedience, and Judah, though equally disobedient, found a glimmer of hope with a young king named Josiah.

Josiah worked to turn Judah back to Yahweh and chose to restore the Temple that had fallen into disrepair. During the renovation, the priest Hilkiah found a scroll and gave it to the king's court secretary, who read it to King Josiah. In response, the king "tore his clothes in despair" (2 Kings 22:11). He then charged Hilkiah and others to go to the Lord and intercede for him and the people, and to find out more about what was written in the scroll.

The text then says, "So Hilkiah the priest, Ahikam, Acbor, Shaphan, and Asaiah went to the New Quarter of Jerusalem to consult with the prophet Huldah. She was the wife of Shallum son of Tikvah, son of Harhas, the keeper of the Temple wardrobe" (2 Kings 22:14).

The significance of Hilkiah consulting Huldah becomes evident when we realize that she had two male contemporaries, Jeremiah and Zephaniah, that Hilkiah could have gone to instead. But Hilkiah didn't choose Jeremiah, also known as the weeping prophet; nor did he choose Zephaniah, who had directly confronted the hypocrisy of Judah's worship. The fact that Hilkiah did not approach either man for counsel and direction says a lot about Huldah and her reputation. Many scholars believe she was a teacher, and the Bible tells us she was also a prophet. I imagine that she faithfully served others day in and day out by sharing wisdom and helping others to know God.

When Huldah spoke on behalf of God to Hilkiah and those who had come with him, she relayed both bad news and good news. The bad news: All the words in the scroll would come true, and the Lord would bring disaster on Jerusalem and her people. The good news: Because of Josiah's humility and repentance, the nation would be spared during the reign of the young king. The promised disaster would not come until after his death.

In the presence of all the people, King Josiah read the scroll that had been found, and both he and the people committed themselves to a renewed covenant with the Lord (2 Kings 23:1-3). He purged the country of false worship by burning down the Asherah poles and burning the chariots dedicated to the sun god. He destroyed the altars used for child sacrifice and executed the priests of the pagan shrines (2 Kings 23:4-20).

Then Josiah reinstated the celebration of Passover:

> There had not been a Passover celebration like that since the time when the judges ruled in Israel, nor throughout all the years of the kings of Israel and Judah. But in the eighteenth year of King Josiah's reign, this Passover was celebrated to the LORD in Jerusalem.
>
> 2 KINGS 23:22-23

Judah was purged of idolatry and brought back to her God and the rightful worship of her Creator.

Huldah had faithfully served her people, and when the time came to proclaim the truth of God and the need for repentance, God used her to help a young king turn an entire nation back to their rightful worship.

God needs women today who will follow in Huldah's footsteps by faithfully learning and speaking the Word of God. In times of destruction and rebellion, there is a need for people to hear the whole gospel—including both the bad news of sin and the good news of redemption.

## Esther

Esther is one of those women who is often quoted and mentioned when it comes to the topic of women in the Bible. Although the book named for her includes no mention of God, the story it tells shouts that God is moving and working even when we can't yet see it. The text makes it clear that Esther is beautiful, but what shines most brightly about this woman is her courage and grace.

Through her sacrifice, God rescued his people from an evil plot to kill them.

Esther was both an exile and an orphan. Following the death of her parents, she was adopted and brought up under the care of her cousin Mordecai. She'd had a pretty rough start in life and then suffered another blow when she was taken from Mordecai and placed in the harem of King Xerxes. Here, her value was measured not by her intellect, personality, or resilience, but by her physical beauty, which would then be exploited as little more than an object. One evening, she dressed herself in the finest handpicked jewels and clothing and was sent to the king's private chambers; the next morning she was sent away, as if her virginity, innocence, and purity meant nothing at all.

The most striking characteristic I see in Esther is her willingness to submit and listen to the wisdom of the men around her while simultaneously walking with both strength and integrity. The text reveals that prior to going into the king, Esther "accepted the advice of Hegai, the eunuch in charge of the harem" and "asked for nothing except what he suggested" (Esther 2:15). She had also adhered to the directive of Mordecai to keep her nationality a secret (Esther 2:10). Even when Xerxes declared her queen and gave great banquets in her honor, she still followed the wisdom of those God placed beside her.

The drama of the story picks up when Mordecai discovers that Haman, one of the king's officials, was plotting to execute all the Jewish people. That's when the fate of Esther's people fell on her shoulders. Mordecai sent her this message:

Don't think for a moment that because you're in the
palace you will escape when all other Jews are killed. If
you keep quiet at a time like this, deliverance and relief

for the Jews will arise from some other place, but you and your relatives will die. Who knows if perhaps you were made queen for just such a time as this?

ESTHER 4:13-14

Most of us would probably go into all-out panic mode at this point, but not Esther. In her moment of stress, she turned to God and prayed. She called for the Jews to pray and fast with her, and her attendants did the same. "And then," she said, "though it is against the law, I will go in to see the king. If I must die, I must die" (Esther 4:16). In God's grace and providence, King Xerxes welcomed her (Esther 5:2). Through a series of dramatic events that followed, Mordecai received a commendation from the king, the evil Haman was exposed and executed, and King Xerxes issued a decree that saved the Jews.

The courage, resilience, and humility Esther displayed to save a nation is yet another example of the Genesis 3:15 promise—that God would bring about redemption for his people—being fulfilled.

Keep in mind that the background of Esther's story is that the king had deposed his first queen, Vashti, because she didn't want to be flaunted at a dinner party (Esther 1:10-12). This angered the king, and his advisors reasoned, "Women everywhere will begin to despise their husbands. . . . There will be no end to their contempt and anger" (Esther 1:17-18). So they concocted a plan to banish Vashti to teach all the wives in the land that they were to listen to and be subject to their husbands. Sounds a lot like a result of the curse we learned about in Genesis 3, doesn't it? The struggle for power, position, and control were the means by which men oppressed women, and God used the strength of a woman to bring about the redemption and freedom of his people. Esther was one of God's *ezers*—the helper, the strong defender, the courageous risk taker—and God was faithfully at work in her story even when he seemed silent.

## Leadership Lessons

In the stories of Deborah, Huldah, and Esther, we see women who were faithful and how God used them at a specific time and within their spheres of influence. All three demonstrate that leadership is not about having a title, people under you, or even telling others what to do. Instead, leadership is a means of using your influence for the betterment of those around you.

Author and leader Jo Saxton said this when she was interviewed about the power of influence:

> When I'm thinking of influence, it's the capacity you have to impact somebody else's life. You can impact the way they think, the conditions they live in, the world they inhabit, the way they perceive themselves. Influence is you shaping somebody else and everybody is shaping someone else. Everyone. You may be shaping them for a moment in impacting their day. You may impact their decade. The way we treat people, the way we speak to people, love people, reject people, empower people, shapes their entire destinies or at least has the potential to. So we are incredibly influential. We often don't remember what [someone] influential in our lives said, as much as who they were. People remember who you [are] to them, the kind of neighbor you are, the kind of colleague you are, the kind of Bible study leader you are, the kind of client you are, the kind of customer you are in a grocery store. We are influencing each other 24/7.[4]

We all have opportunities to influence the people around us every day—from the woman at Target to our children to those we work alongside to the neighbor with the barking dog. The planet is full of souls who are looking for answers. They are looking to be seen in a vast sea of surface relationships and social media expectations. They are looking for steadiness in the midst of constant movement and turnover.

Think of where our three biblical women started out. Deborah was under her palm tree, Huldah was teaching in Jerusalem, Esther was in her cousin's home. I doubt they were thinking God would use them to inspire women for millennia to come. They simply followed God in the moments he had for them, through daily obedience with the people in front of them. And in their faithfulness, God used them to change the course of history.

One final lesson for every woman who aspires to a position of leadership is that each of these women was rooted in the knowledge of Scripture. When the need for strong leadership arises and hardship is bearing down on us, we have to know, cling to, and speak the Word of God. When crisis strikes, we won't have time to do a lengthy study to figure out what God says about how to respond. Just as these three women knew God and his words when war, genocide, and destruction were coming for them and their people, we need to know the promises and power of God so we can be used by him as an extension of that power.

Deborah knew the word of the Lord and rallied the troops to defeat King Jabin and Sisera.

Huldah knew the word of the Lord and inspired King Josiah to institute reforms.

Esther knew the word of the Lord and went to King Xerxes to intercede on behalf of her people, asking him to spare them.

What we know, learn, and believe before we face our crisis

moments in leadership is what will carry us through moments of hardship and trial.

What are you learning about obedience in your everyday life?

What areas of influence do you have in your community, workplace, and church?

Who around you is looking for and needs to hear the truth about God?

What broken systems, ideologies, and abuse is God allowing you to see, change, and bring reform to?

Leadership is about establishing God's Kingdom and his will "on earth, as it is in heaven" (Matthew 6:10). It's about women (and men) leading together in systemic reforms for racial injustice or helping to bridge the gap of poverty in the inner city. It's about leveraging resources to refugees and standing up as protectors of life, from conception onward. Leading with character, integrity, and grit, together we are God's plan A—for such a time as this.

## DISCUSSION QUESTIONS

1. *Do you think of yourself as a leader? If leadership is influence, how does that affect your perspective about owning your leadership potential?*

2. *How have you been valued or undervalued as a woman leader? What opportunities have you been given to use your influence and abilities to speak into decisions, culture, and change?*

3. *Leadership is often something we aspire to, but sometimes we don't think we are equipped or ready for it. Yet we see in the stories of Deborah, Huldah, and Esther that they were faithful in the situations God had placed them in, using them for a bigger impact and purpose in his Kingdom. How does this encourage you in your seasons of obscurity or motivate you to continue being faithful in small platforms?*

4. *Good leadership still models godly submission and wisdom. To lead well, why is it important to maintain deep intimacy with the Lord and time spent in his Word?*

5. *How has unhealthy leadership been modeled to you? What have you learned in those circumstances?*

## 11

# Every Woman Called

**Your Name:**

_____

**Your Story of Meeting Christ:**

_____

_____

_____

_____

_____

_____

_____

_____

_____

_____

_____

**People You Influence:**

_____

_____

_____

_____

_____

_____

_____

_____

_____

_____

_____

_____

_____

**Your Passions:**

_____

_____

_____

_____

_____

_____

_____

_____

_____

_____

_____

_____

_____

_____

_____

_____

**Your Calling:**

_____

_____

_____

_____

_____

_____

_____

_____

_____

_____

_____

_____

——————————— ◉ ———————————

*alling* can be an intimidating and sometimes even mystical word. It's one of those terms that can be thrown around in a variety of contexts and often leaves people feeling either "chosen" or as if they were "just missing the mark." Those who are said to have a calling are seen as somehow special, and the rest of us are just regular people. We think that God does big things only through people who have a special calling, while the rest of us just go about our days paying the bills, caring for the kids, and eating tacos.

Is a calling only for people who feel drawn to vocational (paid) ministry?

Is it a calling when God asks you to do something for him that others haven't been asked to do?

Is a calling always about doing big things, or does it include little things too?

Is a calling for men *and* women?

Is a calling a *feeling*? Is it an audible voice from God?

When I was in my late teens, I had no idea what it would look like for me to surrender to a call to ministry. The only opportunities I had seen for women were to either work overseas in foreign missions or marry a pastor. I also didn't know whether God called women in the same way he called men. In the Bible, there were dramatic stories of God calling men—for example, Moses through a burning bush and Paul by striking him blind along the side of a road—but I didn't see similar stories of God calling women.

There was no physical manifestation of God in front of me telling me what to do, where to go, or how to serve. Neither was there an older, more mature woman in front of me showing me how to walk or forge the path ahead of me.

And yet, for my male peers, having a calling seemed to be so clear cut. And that's because it often was. Consider the contrast evident in this story from a sister in ministry: As a young woman, she wanted to devote her life to ministry but had no idea what to do. When she approached her pastor after a Sunday service, he prayed for her and sent her on her way. A few weeks later, a young man who sensed a similar call to ministry approached the pastor during a time of prayer in the service. The pastor not only prayed for him but also announced the young man's calling and celebrated it at the end of the service. But that's not all; the young man became a pastoral intern at the church, immediately gained the congregation's support, and was gifted a small amount of funding when he went to seminary.

In contrast, the young woman volunteered in the student ministry and began leading Bible studies. She went on to marry a pharmacist, raise three boys, and put herself through seminary. She is now pursuing her doctorate. Was she any less called than the young man who had such a different experience? Of course not.

But as a woman, she received no support or affirmation from her pastor or church, no encouragement to discern or follow God's call on her life.

I didn't walk down the church aisle like my friend did, but I had some conversations with my pastor about what the Lord was teaching me and stirring in me. I shared with him how much I loved being involved in the church and my heart for people.

Believing that God wanted me to make some changes in my life, I prayed about it and talked to my parents, then made the decision to stop pursuing a biology degree at the University of Texas at Dallas and enrolled instead at Criswell College, a tiny Bible college where my pastor was a professor. No burning bush, no flash from heaven. Just a small act of obedience and surrender—to learn as much as I could about the Bible—and a sizable determination *not* to marry a preacher. (God had other plans.)

Some may push back and say, "Things are going to look different for those who are stepping into vocational ministry and those who aren't." But I would argue that, by placing so much emphasis on "vocational ministry" as a "calling," we may completely overlook and silence the general call for *all* believers to live out their lives as sons or daughters of God who are *on mission* for his Kingdom.

I've had many conversations with women of all ages who feel called but are wrestling through what it looks like for them to follow God. Should they go to seminary? What job opportunities are open to women in their denomination? Should they quit their jobs to go work in a paid ministry position at a church? One woman told me she had studied to be a schoolteacher but had never felt called to children's ministry—which seemed to be the only avenue open to her at her church—so she thought she couldn't be a leader, even though she had *decades* of experience in both vocational and church contexts that would make her a phenomenal leader.

When our conversations about *calling* focus primarily on paid ministry positions, and when there are few such positions where a woman can identify, develop, and use her gifts, we end up with a whole bunch of women who feel unqualified and limited in the local church.

## Called to Salvation

In his first letter to the church at Corinth, the apostle Paul uses the Greek word *klētos* (meaning "called"), or related words, seven times in the first chapter alone. *Klētos* means "a call or invitation," such as to a feast or celebration. It is also used "in a technical sense, [as] the divine invitation to embrace salvation in the kingdom of God."[1]

In his letter to the church at Ephesus, Paul writes, "I, a prisoner for serving the Lord, beg you to lead a life worthy of your calling, for you have been called by God" (Ephesians 4:1). In speaking of *calling*, Paul isn't addressing only the elders of the church, only the men, or only the Jewish believers. He is talking to all believers— everyone who has been called, chosen, adopted, and redeemed.

All who are redeemed have been called.

All who are called are commanded to minister.

But not all who are called are gifted to lead.

Each of us who has been saved and redeemed by the work of Jesus has been called, so the question isn't *if* we are called, but instead *where* and *how* we are called to minister.

## Called and Commissioned

Seed Company and Barna Research recently conducted a study to assess what Christians think about missions and other biblical worldview issues. Among their findings was this:

When asked if they had previously "heard of the Great Commission," half of U.S. churchgoers (51%) say they do not know this term. It would be reassuring to assume that the other half who know the term are also actually familiar with the passage known by this name, but that proportion is low (17%). Meanwhile, "the Great Commission" does ring a bell for one in four (25%), though they can't remember what it is.[2]

Jesus never used the term *Great Commission*. It is simply the designation given to this charge to his disciples right before his ascension: "Go and make disciples of all the nations, baptizing them in the name of the Father and the Son and the Holy Spirit" (Matthew 28:19). So the concerning thing about the survey finding isn't so much that people don't know the term itself, but that they don't know what it means. Across the church, men and women haven't been taught what it means to be a disciple and join in the mission of God as one who is called. Once again, there is a disconnect between our orthodoxy (what we believe about God) and our orthopraxy (how we live out that belief).

You and I are not just called to be forgiven of our sins so that one day we can go to heaven. If that were the goal, Jesus could have taken us to glory in the moment of our justification. Instead, he justifies and saves us so that we can join him in the mission to reach everyone on the planet with the good news that they, too, are created in God's image and need him for salvation.

So if you and I are included in what it means to be called, what are we supposed to be doing as called women? I want to address that by unpacking four phrases from the Great Commission itself:

Jesus came and told his disciples, "I have been given all authority in heaven and on earth. *Therefore, go* and *make disciples* of all the nations, *baptizing them* in the name of the Father and the Son and the Holy Spirit. *Teach* these new disciples to obey all the commands I have given you. And be sure of this: I am with you always, even to the end of the age."

MATTHEW 28:18-20, ITALICS ADDED

### *"Therefore, Go"*

Many of us tend to think the first step in being *called* and *sent out* is to sit in a classroom and learn all the basic doctrines and gain a right understanding of Jesus' teachings. I often hear from women that they don't feel qualified to lead because they don't know enough, or they can't serve in a certain area because they may not know the answer to someone's question. As Jesus gathered his disciples, he didn't assemble the smartest, most influential, or most educated group of guys. He called an assortment of people with different vocations and personalities who were in varying life stages and then lived life with them for three years. Jesus doesn't start with how much you *know*; he starts with *go*. Going has more to do with your mindset and intentionality in your everyday moments than it does with completing an educational process or program. *Go* is the motivation behind our work, relationships, and to-do lists. And *going* may include mundane, everyday activities such as

- picking up your kids at school;
- leading a board meeting;
- meeting for coffee with a neighbor or the local PTA moms;
- taking a walk through your neighborhood; and
- posting on social media.

As you *go*, make known the Kingdom of God.

### "Make Disciples"

To be a disciple means to be a learner or a pupil of a teacher. In Jesus' day, disciples were often associated with their teacher, and so, for example, they would be called disciples of John or disciples of Apollos. Discipleship, then, is not only about the position of being a student of a teacher, but also about the relationship and identification with that teacher.

In the words of the late author and pastor Eugene Peterson, "Christian discipleship is a decision to walk in his ways, steadily and firmly, and then finding that the way integrates all our interests, passions and gifts, our human needs and our eternal aspirations. It is the way of life we were created for."[3]

Simply put, if we are making disciples, we are connecting them to and bringing them under the wisdom, teaching, and example of Jesus. But Jesus also notes a couple of distinctions that characterize what it means to make disciples: We are to baptize and teach them.

### "Baptizing Them"

Some of my favorite Sunday church services are when we have baptisms. The person who is being baptized is asked to confirm that they have surrendered their life to Jesus, and their personality shines through with either a quiet yes or a loud and emphatic yes. Then the minister will say something along the lines of, "I baptize you, my sister [or my brother], in the name of the Father, Son, and Holy Spirit."

Baptism is so much more than getting wet; it is a public declaration of being birthed into a new family of brothers and sisters, all in reflection of the relationships within the Trinity. It is a symbol of dying to self and our enmity with God and being reborn and adopted into a new family. The relational implications of our being created in God's image are then lived out within the context of a local church, where we are to practice the "one anothers" of Scripture.[4]

### *"Teach"*

Teaching may sound intimidating to some. In a digital age when we can google everything from how to cook a potato in the microwave to how to self-diagnose a strange abdominal pain, we have access to a world of information, and yet people are more lost than ever when it comes to the fundamental truths of who they are, why they matter, and what their purpose is.

When I'm talking with women, I often hear statements like "I don't know enough to disciple someone" or "I wasn't discipled myself, so what if I teach something wrong?" We imagine a high academic bar that requires us to use big theological words, and we shrink back in fear, thinking we don't have anything to offer anyone.

Psalm 119, the longest in the book of Psalms, contains vital truths about the Word of God and its richness in our lives. It reflects the importance of having a life that is set on the Word of God. The psalmist writes,

> You made me; you created me.
>     Now give me the sense to follow your commands.
> May all who fear you find in me a cause for joy,
>     for I have put my hope in your word.

PSALM 119:73-74

The heartbeat of the believer is the work of the Spirit through the power and revelation of the Word of God, and we must be willing to walk alongside others to explain the truth of God's words, especially in a world that is full of deception and lies.

There is a deep need for women who are willing to open their homes and sacrifice their time to come alongside others and talk with them about life, friendships, marriage, and faith. We need only to look to the life of Jesus to see how he taught his disciples and lived life with them. They traveled together, ate meals together, and journeyed together through grief and joy in different seasons of life. He didn't bring them into a classroom, but he used everyday images and activities—like a fig tree, a coin, and fishing—to teach them about the Kingdom of God.

Who are you coming alongside that you can teach to consider and embrace the things of God?

## Trust in the One Who Is With You

As we seek to live out the Great Commission, it's important to remember that we don't have to do it alone. Remember, Jesus said, "Be sure of this: I am with you always, even to the end of the age" (Matthew 28:20). That's a promise that still blows my mind. Jesus also promised to send the Holy Spirit to reside within us (John 14:26). That promise was fulfilled at Pentecost (Acts 2:1-4). The Holy Spirit's work in us is to make us more like Jesus, to empower us to be the reflections of God to a broken world, and to help us enable the people around us to know and be known by God, allowing them to flourish. This is the Great Commission.

The fact that God is with us is such a liberating truth. Instead of trying to muster up wisdom and understanding we don't have, we can rely on the Holy Spirit for guidance, direction, and conviction and move with the same power that Jesus himself modeled while he walked the planet.

We can also be encouraged by the promise that the Holy Spirit has given each of us unique gifts that reflect the beauty and work of God. Wisdom, knowledge, faith, service, generosity, prophecy, and teaching are just a few of the gifts that the Spirit of God imparts to believers (see Romans 12:6-8; 1 Corinthians 12:8-10). These spiritual gifts are for the encouragement, edification, and equipping of the church and for sharing the gospel as we are sent out.

It is easy for us to assume that evangelism, or sharing Jesus, is only for those who work vocationally at a church. We might think of missionaries and pastors as the ones who are *called* to be on the front lines of ministry, while the rest of us hold down secular jobs and manage our families. We dissect and compartmentalize, when the metanarrative of Scripture is clear that all who are redeemed by the work of Jesus are also sent by Jesus.

We are to be salt and light (Matthew 5:13-16).

We are to be a city on a hill (Matthew 5:14).

We are to hunger and thirst for justice (Matthew 5:6).

We are to live with integrity (Proverbs 20:7).

We are to use our influence for the good of our neighbors—sometimes at the expense of ourselves (Philippians 2:3-4).

We are to share our homes and invite in the stranger (Matthew 25:35).

If we have been adopted into the family of God, we have had the privilege and the joy of being able to spread the hope and good news of salvation that turned our lives upside down in the best of ways. We are to be a reflection of what God has done for us in pursuing us, graciously redeeming us, and calling us his own.

I love how the apostle Peter encouraged those who were being persecuted:

God has given each of you a gift from his great variety
of spiritual gifts. Use them well to serve one another. Do
you have the gift of speaking? Then speak as though God
himself were speaking through you. Do you have the gift
of helping others? Do it with all the strength and energy
that God supplies. Then everything you do will bring
glory to God through Jesus Christ. All glory and power to
him forever and ever! Amen.

I PETER 4:10-11

Just as Peter encouraged his brothers and sisters by asking
about their gifts, the same question is being asked of you. How
has the Spirit gifted you? Where do your passions, story, and spiritual gifts align for the glory of God? How are you intentionally
being salt, light, truth, and grace to fulfill the prayer, "May your
Kingdom come soon. May your will be done on earth, as it is in
heaven" (Matthew 6:10)? Whatever your gift, exercise it with all
the strength and energy that God supplies.

## Where Do I Start?

You may be thinking, *I know that I am called. I know that I am sent.
But what now? Where do I start?*

Great questions! Here are four ideas to get you started.

1. **Write out your story.** Your story is one of the most unique
   and valuable tools that God has given you to share the
   power of the gospel. A specific culture, time, and place
   made all the women we have studied who they were. They
   had different struggles and obstacles that God used to help
   grow them in character and faith.

   As you think of your unique story—including your

family, the hardships you've walked through, and how God has extended grace to you in those times—write down what comes to mind. One model for writing out your story of surrendering to Jesus is to think of it in three parts: *before* Jesus, *meeting* Jesus, and *after* Jesus. Write out who you were before you surrendered to Jesus, how you met Jesus and gave your life to him, and then how your life changed afterward.

2. **Take a spiritual-gifts assessment.** There are plenty of books and online resources that can help you identify what your spiritual gifts might be. Most ask a series of questions to home in on how God has gifted you. One I often recommend is the Team Ministry Spiritual Gifts Inventory (see https://gifts.churchgrowth.org/spiritual-gifts-survey). Whatever assessment you choose, identify your top three gifts and then look for opportunities to use those gifts.

3. **Serve, and serve some more.** Trial and error was a big part of how I learned what I was good at, and perhaps even more importantly, what I wasn't good at. Many of us tend to have ideas in our heads of what we are supposed to be or what our calling is supposed to look like, and it isn't until we get our hands dirty and rub shoulders with others in the trenches that we discover with clarity what our gifts and abilities actually are.

For a season, I taught our church's three- to four-year-olds class each Sunday. I thought that because my kids were that age and I loved to teach, it would be a great way to serve and invest in the next generation. I failed miserably! Three- and four-year-olds do not want to sit still listening to a Bible story, nor do they care what a Bible word means in its original language. Although I do have the gift of teaching, I learned that I needed to have a slightly older audience. Even more than that, I developed a greater appreciation for those who were gifted to bring the Bible to life in creative and interactive ways for children.

4. **Start small and be faithful.** In a culture that seems to value only big titles and big platforms, it is easy for us to think that we have to do something big in order to serve Jesus. And it may be that he is calling you to do something big. But for most, he is calling us to be faithful with what he has already given.

If you are like me, you run out of the gate full steam ahead and commit to serving at the food pantry, leading a Bible study, and discipling five college students—and then you realize you're dropping the ball in every other area of life. Instead, take an inventory of where you have influence and start there. Following Jesus isn't an added item on your to-do list; it is a transformation of *who you are* as you live your life. My encouragement is to set one goal and take one step out of your comfort zone. Then watch what God does with a willing heart and open hands.

## Ignite Your Inspiration

We have covered a lot in this book about how God has used women throughout redemptive history. I hope that as you read about these women, you found yourself reflected in their stories. I also hope that you are asking the question, "So what do I do now?"—because the simple answer is "Go."

The Great Commission isn't just for our brothers in Christ, but for all who have been called, redeemed, and made new by the work of Jesus Christ through the Holy Spirit. If you are a woman who has surrendered her life to Jesus, then you, too, are a part of a long lineage of faithful women called to live out the Great Commission.

So often we try to compartmentalize our lives into the categories of our work, families, and hobbies. We treat the will of God as if it were a puzzle in which we have to perfectly piece together every aspect of our lives. Then we wonder whether we'll feel like we have finally arrived, whether we'll find fulfillment even if all the pieces were to fit perfectly together.

Maybe we have been looking at this thing completely backward. Instead of asking, "How does every area of my life fit together in this puzzle of God's will," we should ask, "Who am I? How do I reflect my Creator?" These questions go far deeper than how you and I earn a paycheck, and they tap into our God-given passions and purpose.

The answer to who we are far transcends where we call home, what family we were born into, and whether we are introverted or extroverted, strong-willed or passive. For you and for me, the answer begins with a good God who chose to breathe life, creativity, and distinction into every woman, beginning with a woman named Eve and continuing throughout history to the women you and I are today.

God's story is still being written. This book is filled with the stories of ordinary women God used—sometimes in everyday ways and sometimes in extraordinary ways—to inspire, lead, protect, and change the course of history. He used them for the good of others and for his glory.

God has uniquely made you, gifted you, and empowered you with his good design.

Did your heart beat a little faster as you read stories of women you can relate to whom God has used to further his Kingdom?

Did you recall the names of people who need to hear the Good News or remember areas of service you've dreamed about stepping into?

Do you feel encouraged to accept your call to live out the Great Commission?

Stepping confidently into your calling requires listening to God's voice, surrendering your fears and insecurities—no matter how big or small—and saying with your life that God is who he says he is.

The God who has used women all throughout redemptive history is the same God who is calling and commissioning you and me today.

He's calling. Let's go!

## DISCUSSION QUESTIONS

1. Which woman from the Bible has inspired you most? What about her story resonates with you?

2. What women in your life have modeled what it means to be a disciple? How have their stories or giftings encouraged you in your own journey?

3. In what ways, if any, have you shrunk back from what God has called you to do or be? What fears keep you from walking forward in confidence?

4. In what ways do you feel drawn to use and develop your gifts?

5. What is one step of obedience you are taking to live out your calling in your local context?

# Notes

## 1: SEARCHING FOR WOMANHOOD
1. C. S. Lewis, *The Lion, the Witch and the Wardrobe* (Boston: Wyatt North, 2018), n.p.

## 2: MADE IN HIS IMAGE
1. Hannah Anderson, email correspondence with the author.
2. Kenneth A. Mathews, *The New American Commentary*, Genesis 1-11:26, vol. 1A (Nashville: B&H, 1996). Retrieved from https://app.wordsearchbible.com.

## 3: WOMEN AND SINGLENESS
1. Lina Abujamra, *Thrive: The Single Life as God Intended* (Chicago: Moody, 2013), 20–21.

## 4: WOMEN AND MARRIAGE
1. Elisabeth Elliot, *Suffering Is Never for Nothing* (Nashville: B&H, 2019), 12.
2. Timothy Keller with Kathy Keller, *The Meaning of Marriage* (New York: Penguin, 2011), 100–101.

## 6: WOMEN AND WORK
1. Stephanie Kaplan Lewis, "Glamour's 20 Amazing Young Women Who Are Already Changing the World," HuffPost Contributor blog, May 25, 2011, https://www.huffpost.com/entry/glamours-20-amazing-young_b_787106.
2. "2016 30 Under 30: Media," *Forbes*, January 4, 2016, www.forbes.com/pictures/flji45ffil/zim-ugochukwu-27/?sh=7af960526c7c.
3. Alisa Gumbs, "25 Black Women Who Are Changing the World," *Black Enterprise*, March 28, 2018, https://www.blackenterprise.com/image

-gallery-black-women-changing-the-world/; "The World's Most Innovative Companies 2016: Travel Honorees," *Fast Company*, accessed December 3, 2021, https://www.fastcompany.com/most-innovative -companies/2016/sectors/travel.

4. "Meet the SuperSoul100: The World's Biggest Trailblazers In One Room," Oprah.com, https://www.oprah.com/spirit/supersoul100-the-worlds -biggest-trailblazers-in-one-room.

5. Zim Flores, interview with Shari Noland, "Dare to Bloom," Urban Faith, December 9, 2020, https://urbanfaith.com/tag/zim-flores/.

6. Zim Flores, *Dare to Bloom: Trusting God through Painful Endings and New Beginnings* (Nashville: Thomas Nelson, 2020), 36.

7. You can read more of Zim's story at https://www.zimism.com.

8. "100 Years of Working Women," Women's Bureau, US Department of Labor, accessed November 23, 2021, https://www.dol.gov/agencies/wb /data/occupations-decades-100.

9. Herbert Lockyer, "Lydia," in *All the Women of the Bible* (Grand Rapids, MI: Zondervan, 1988), 84; also accessed November 24, 2021, https:// www.biblegateway.com/resources/all-women-bible/Lydia.

### 7: WOMEN AND MISSION

1. Karen Watson, quoted in Erich Bridges and Jerry Rankin, *Lives Given, Not Taken: 21st-Century Southern Baptist Martyrs* (Richmond, VA: International Mission Board, SBC, 2005), 191–192.

2. D. A. Carson, ed., *The Gospel according to John* (Grand Rapids, MI: Eerdmans, 1991), 216.

### 8: WOMEN AND THE CHURCH

1. Beth Moore, interview with Russell Moore, "Beth Moore Didn't Expect Us to Be Us," *Russell Moore Show* podcast, episode 1, October 6, 2021, https://www.christianitytoday.com/ct/podcasts/russell-moore-show /russell-moore-and-beth-moore-live-in-nashville.html.

2. See, for example, Allan Chapple, "Getting *Romans* to the Right Romans: Phoebe and the Delivery of Paul's Letter," *Tyndale Bulletin*, November 1, 2011, https://tyndalebulletin.org/article/29314.

### 9: WOMEN AND JUSTICE FOR THE VULNERABLE

1. "Read Rachael Denhollander's Full Victim Impact Statement about Larry Nassar," CNN, January 30, 2018, https://www.cnn.com/2018/01/24/us /rachael-denhollander-full-statement/index.html.

2. Daniel A. Biddle, *The Secret of the Seven Pillars: Building Your Life on God's Wisdom from the Book of Proverbs* (Maitland, FL: Xulon, 2007), 112.

3. "Slavery by the Numbers," A21 website, accessed December 3, 2021, https://www.a21.org/content/human-trafficking/gqe0rc.

## 10: WOMEN AND LEADERSHIP

1. Jenny Yang, email correspondence with the author, October 10, 2021.
2. Yang, email correspondence.
3. Herbert Lockyer, "Deborah No. 2," in *All the Women of the Bible*, (Grand Rapids, MI: Zondervan, 1988), 41, also accessed November 26, 2021, https://www.biblegateway.com/resources/all-women-bible/Deborah-No-2.
4. Jo Saxton, interview by Jennie Allen, "Stop Hiding Your Gifts with Jo Saxton," *#madeforthispodcast*, April 21, 2020, https://premierespeakers .com/christian/jennie_allen/posts/top_hiding_your_gifts_with_jo_saxton.

## 11. EVERY WOMAN CALLED

1. *Thayer's Greek Lexicon*, electronic database, copyright © 2002, 2003, 2006, 2011 by Biblesoft, Inc. All rights reserved. Used by permission. Biblesoft.com.
2. "51% of Churchgoers Don't Know about the Great Commission," Barna, March 27, 2018, https://www.barna.com/research/half-churchgoers-not -heard-great-commission/.
3. Eugene H. Peterson, *A Long Obedience in the Same Direction* (Downers Grove, IL: InterVarsity, 2021), 128.
4. For a list of fifty-nine "one another" verses in the Bible, see storage .cloversites.com/wakarusamissionarychurch/documents/59one_another _scriptures.pdf.

# About the Author

JACKI C. KING is a respected and popular Bible teacher, conference speaker, and ministry leader. She has a passion for seeing women fall in love with Jesus and his Word while challenging them to be on mission in their homes, workplaces, and communities. Jacki is a native Texan who now lives in central Arkansas with her husband, Josh, a lead pastor, and their three boys. Jacki holds a bachelor's degree in biblical studies and ministry to women from Criswell College and a master of arts in theological studies from Southwestern Baptist Theological Seminary.

If you liked this book, you'll want to get involved in

# Church Member Equip!

—
—

Do you have a desire to learn more about serving God through your local church?

Would you like to see how God can use you in new and exciting ways?

Get your church involved in Church Member Equip, an online ministry designed to prepare church leaders and church members to better serve God's mission and purpose.

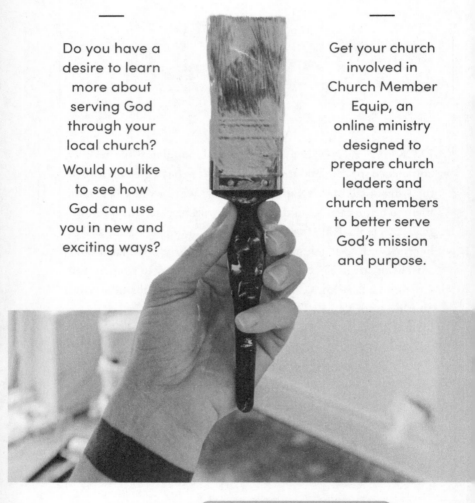

Check us out at   **www.ChurchMemberEquip.com**

**CHURCH ANSWERS**
FEATURING THOM RAINER

CP1749